Dianne

Advance praise for *Between Two Trailers*

"*Between Two Trailers* is a love story of brokenness and heart-wrenching pain, all wrapped up in reconciliation that will invite readers to pause and consider the places where we are holding on to pain that isn't ours to carry."

—KARLA KAMSTRA, TikTok personality, author of *Untangling*

"I was gripped by the first gorgeous and terrifying line and could not put the book down. We walk with J. Dana Trent as she navigates a childhood of potentially suffocating factors of mental health, poverty, and a drug ring, to eventually explore themes of family and home, all while keeping it as messy and heart-wrenching as surviving and healing truly is. She does not flinch in the face of overwhelming pain and complexity, but rather offers a nuanced narrative full of uncommon warmth and grace. Trent and her story are truly remarkable."

—ELLIE ROSCHER, author of *The Embodied Path*

"J. Dana Trent gives flesh to words we sometimes use lightly: *redemption, hope, miracle, legacy, home*. So much more than prizes for having survived astonishing pain, these words and their stories are born of an even more astonishing grace. In her willingness to enter both the pain and the grace, Trent illuminates the fractured treasures—not to fix them, but to bear witness to their part in a life that is whole."

—JAN RICHARDSON, author of *Sparrow*

"Trent's drug-dealing father ('King') and emotional mess of a mother ('The Lady') laughingly, maddeningly goofed up so many times during their crazy crash lives. But one thing these two got right: By the grace of God, they bumbled into giving us a daughter who knows how to tell their story in a way that's believably beguiling, outrageous, revealing, tender, true, sad, and funny, all at the same time. Trent's is a memoir you'll always remember."

—WILL WILLIMON, professor of the practice of Christian ministry at Duke Divinity School, author of *Accidental Preacher*

"J. Dana Trent's memoir is a carnival of drug dealing, alcoholism, mental illness, and 1970s televangelism, all seen through the wide eyes of a child and young adult. A self-described 'midfielder' between two dysfunctional parents, Trent's voice rarely judges and never wavers. She not only survives her childhood but somehow makes it 'home' to a settled peace with her history. Her story is a literary barn burner."

—RICHARD LISCHER, author of *Our Hearts Are Restless*

"In a world of half-truths, shiny social media posts, and projections of perfectionism, Trent's memoir offers us an alternative of wholeness. With profound transparency, she tells us the truth about her own life and invites us to do the same. What can heal our souls, she offers in *Between Two Trailers*, is simply this: to come out of hiding."

—ELIZABETH HAGAN, author of *Brave Church*

"This is a book of miracles, the greatest of which may be the author's capacity to transform a dirt-true human story into hope. J. Dana Trent relates a broken history with integrity, grace, and welcome."

—ROSALIND C. HUGHES, author of *A Family Like Mine*

BETWEEN
TWO
TRAILERS

BETWEEN TWO TRAILERS

A Memoir

J. DANA TRENT

CONVERGENT
NEW YORK

Published in the United States by Convergent Books, an imprint of Random House, a division of Penguin Random House LLC, New York.

CONVERGENT BOOKS is a registered trademark and the Convergent colophon is a trademark of Penguin Random House LLC.

LIBRARY OF CONGRESS CATALOGING-IN-PUBLICATION DATA
Names: Trent, J. Dana, author.
Title: Between two trailers / J. Dana Trent.
Description: First edition. | New York, NY: Convergent Books, 2024
Identifiers: LCCN 2023048678 (print) | LCCN 2023048679 (ebook) |
ISBN 9780593444078 (hardcover) | ISBN 9780593444085 (ebook)
Subjects: LCSH: Children of drug addicts—United States. |
Drug addicts—Family relationships—United States. | Women
clergy—United States.
Classification: LCC HV5824.C45 T75 2024 (print) |
LCC HV5824.C45 (ebook) |
DDC 362.29/13092 [B]—dc23/eng/20240125
LC record available at https://lccn.loc.gov/2023048678
LC ebook record available at https://lccn.loc.gov/2023048679

Printed in the United States of America on acid-free paper

convergentbooks.com

2 4 6 8 9 7 5 3 1

First Edition

Book design by Susan Turner

For Achilles, Leuge, Marietta, Lindah, and Doggy:
I would not have survived without you.

And for G&GL: Thank you for bringing me back home.

Finally, with gratitude for my dad and mom, who instilled
in me a love of home, no matter where I find it.

by Barbara Brown Taylor

HERE'S SOMETHING VERY FEW PEOPLE KNOW ABOUT writing a book: If everything works out, other people are going to read it. That story inside of you that wanted out—the true one that has you right in the middle of it—is finally going to find its wings. You're going to lose the heavy narrative weight of it. Those who read it are going to rise with your assurance that they are not the only ones with secrets like yours, and because you have told yours with such grit and grace, they are going to consider what relief there might be in telling theirs too.

So you work and work on this book, practicing the delicate surgery of telling your story without invading other people's stories. When this turns out to be impossible, you do the moral math. Will the number of people you hurt be less than or equal to the number of people you help? How do the virtues of telling the whole story stack up against the virtues of holding back? You can always create composite characters or change basic details so readers can't identify the solo actors, but if the solo actors read or hear about the book, they will be able to identify themselves. So will everyone else close to your story. While you're not sleeping at night, you imagine being in the same room with them when they let your book fall into their laps and say, "I can't believe you wrote that about me."

If you finish writing the book, that's your evidence that you believe the story is worth telling. If your book finds a publisher, that's your sign that other people believe it too. This huge blast of confidence lasts all the way to the day you receive the page proofs from your editor—the ones you're meant to check for errors and make final changes on before it's too late. There's something about seeing your story laid out like that, with all the copyright information at the front, a formal table of contents, and page numbers on all the pages, that can liquify your guts.

All of a sudden, you're reading this thing you wrote and realize what's coming: first reviews, sales reports, Amazon stars and Goodreads bars, followed by messages from long-ago friends and distant relatives who just heard about it and can't wait to read it. *Why wasn't any of this real to you before?* With any luck, a lot of people are going to read this book. *That's what you wanted, right?* It's certainly what your publisher wants, which is why you're going to get a great many opportunities to talk openly about this very intimate, very spiky story you have worked years to write down. All that time it was just the two of you on a desert island, and now here comes the cruise ship.

Dana Trent was one of my heroes even before she wrote this book. She has written others, which sparkle with her gift for saying hard things with intelligence and humor. When you

meet her, you can sense that same energetic willingness to
look straight at real life and say something true about it that
you can swallow even if it takes two or three tries. But she has
never written a book like this. In this one, she who has taken
such care with other people's stories has accepted the very
great risk of telling her own. She has done it for herself, certainly, but she has done it for you and me too, to remind us
that there is more at work in all of our stories than any of us
knows. Wounds and blessings come in matched pairs, at least
if we're willing to wrestle them to the ground. That's not a
promise; it's a dare, and the only way to find out what hap-
pens next is to accept.

Barbara Brown Taylor
Clarkesville, Georgia

Story Shrapnel

HOOSIERS ARE NOT TEXANS. OUR STORIES DON'T UNFURL in molasses-thick accents and *Dallas* tough-guy tapestries. Indiana is the land of *Stranger Things* and methamphetamine, not Mary Karr and moonshine jars. A solid Corn Belt story is as dusty as a grain elevator at harvest. We refuse tidy narratives because archives are for rich people, which we are not. We are raccoons, not raconteurs, spewing scraps of Americana alongside rusted trash barrels. Our listeners urgently piece together whose son stabbed whose brother at whose dining room table, because the culprit may be staring right at you. He may even be your own kin.

From gossip to family lore, the oral history of my home-town and namesake—Dana, Indiana—is told in story shrapnel. It's scattered in burnt minefields of time lines and spent bullets, where wounded characters echo across Vermillion County. Ask too much—you'll get a war. Ask nothing—you'll get more.

Indiana's landlocked erraticism creates the kind of culture that births steel courage like Ernie Pyle's. A Pulitzer Prize–winning Hoosier and patron saint of frontline war stories, Ernie came from this lush land of cornfields that offers America food it loves—and people it loves to disdain.

A battlefield is, after all, a *place*. It's dirt and people and weapons and stories. It's wounds and rage. These pages are filled with the casings of blown-up lives. Herein is a true story, one that is at its best when uncovering healing in the very places where violence thrives.

This is a book for anyone who thinks they can't go home.

| CONTENTS |

T HIS IS MY STORY, TOLD TO THE BEST OF MY ABILITY
through the lens of what I remember. Events are described from memories and corroborated by letters,
photos, journal entries, medical records, military records,
court records, and interviews. Names and identifying details
of many living characters have been changed and/or compos-
ited to disguise identities. Some time lines have been shifted
and combined for the reader's ease, for clarity, and to provide
further confidentiality. Any resulting resemblance to other
persons living or deceased that has ensued from these changes
and/or composites is coincidental and unintentional.

The exceptions are my deceased parents, King and the
Lady, whose complicated lives are depicted here with authen-
ticity and empathy.

PART I

I'm sitting down at my desk at school . . . and my mind is beginning to drift off toward home. A person never really misses a little town such as Dana until he's actually away for a while.

—Rick "King" Lewman, Douglas, Georgia
Letter to the Editor, *The Dana News,*
Dana, Indiana, Fall 1965

ONE

Razor Blades and Preschoolers

A PRESCHOOLER'S HANDS ARE THE PERFECT SIZE FOR razor blades. I know because I helped my schizo-phrenic drug-lord father chop, drop, and traffic kilos in kiddie carnival-ride carcasses across flyover country.

In the 1980s, our family business was working for a big drug boss named Viper, buying and selling drugs. My parents were broke—educated but jobless, capable but troubled. My father had unemployed time on his hands and a constant de-pendence on mind-altering substances, so he turned to the pastime he knew in and out: street pharmaceuticals. That's when Viper found him and recruited him to serve as regional manager for a trafficking front called Carnival Captivations. My father had graduated to the big leagues.

Along with his drug boss, my father used kiddie-ride card-board boxes and fiberglass carcasses to move drugs across the country. These hydraulic ponies turned out to be the perfect mules. With each drop, we unloaded inventory and transformed bland Kmart entrances into mini carnivals that boasted dollar-generating rides for young children.

An inexhaustible supply of marijuana bales and cocaine bricks occupied our single-wide trailer alongside Dad, Mom, and me. Drugs were funneled to us by Viper, who organized drops and headed the kiddie-ride business. Dad's entourage were loyal men with street names that reflected their personalities or vices. Together with them, our little family supplied midwesterners with enough uppers and downers to soothe the monotony of landlocked Vermillion County.

I was eighteen months old when we moved twenty minutes south from a trailer in my paternal grandparents' yard in my namesake of Dana, Indiana (population six hundred), to the brand-new single wide on Ninth Street in Clinton (population five thousand). My mom, Judy Trent, and my dad, Rick Lewman, bought the Ninth Street trailer on credit in the early 1980s after going broke in L.A. It came standard with white-and-brown lace curtains and formaldehyde. Mom called it a shotgun house because if our enemies spent twelve-gauge buckshot through the kitchen window, we'd drop like dominoes.

Our new trailer sat on a rented lot of weeds poking up through sparse gravel, twenty minutes from my father's parents, my aunt and uncle, and my two cousins. Across the pot-holed blacktop, I watched corn grow taller than Larry Bird by Labor Day.

My earliest memories of that trailer are of the skunky smell of marijuana and the dull shine of razor blades scattered across the scratched kitchen counter.

Dad was known in Vermillion County as a cult leader. Everyone called him "King." Lore had it that Dad had earned the street name playing one of Shakespeare's title characters in his Vermillion County high school play. But I knew by the way he answered the phone—"Talk to me!"—that he was King of *all* play. He was the one you called when you were down and wanted to be up.

Back then, his long bushy beard was still black. Tall, olive-skinned, and potbellied from cirrhosis of the liver, he commanded our living room like a fire-and-brimstone preacher holding forth from a pulpit. In his signature dirty overalls, he cast his manic "veeshuns" (visions) into smoke clouds, a congregation of devoted gang members gathered to hear the prophecies. They were loyal, attentive disciples with weathered faces whose given names I never knew. Dad, too busy to bother with me before I could walk, used duct tape to fasten my hands to my baby bottle filled with chocolate milk. I sat on the kitchen counter by him all day, lifting that duct-taped bottle to my mouth and catching his marijuana exhales as weed ash fell onto his open King James Bible.

My mother, whom we called "the Lady," smoked joints in bed in the trailer's back bedroom while binge-watching *The 700 Club* on the Christian Broadcasting Network. She was only in her forties but was in a constant state of depression and anxiety. "Your mother's never satisfied," King said once when we were chopping at the counter. "It's ah-lah-way-es some-a-thing," he added in his best Gilda Radner impression. The Lady stayed sprawled out on the king-sized bed they'd bought on layaway. She wasn't sick or inept or in need of a hiatus. She just fancied herself Victorian royalty, lounging around braless with sagging breasts in dirty sheets and a holey T-shirt that read, "I Believe in Miracles!"

"Help the poor," she'd shout when she was hungry. We took her food on bed trays usually reserved for children with chicken pox or broken legs. In bed, she scribbled marginalia on the pages of *How to Win Friends and Influence People* and *What Color Is Your Parachute?* And she cried through Tammy Faye Bakker's earnest pleas for a hurting world. Unfinished "Now I Lay Me Down to Sleep" cross-stitch patterns were strewn across the bed, her stained sheets piled high with textiles. But the Lady never seemed to mind smoking King's inventory. In that trailer, she was a sitting duck who didn't even know how to pull the trigger of the Glock that Viper made us tuck away in a rust-colored pillowcase. Instead, the Lady relied on King's wild threats of knife-slicing and disemboweling his enemies, which had gotten him that far. Her cocktail of benzos and weed—and a passive death wish—didn't hurt either.

I was holed up with her and King all the time, a witness to their moods and reclusiveness, their isolation galvanized by depression and the drug business. By age four, I'd been expelled from preschool for peeling the paint off the walls after leading nap-time coups. So, instead of teaching me my ABC's, King trained me up hustling, giving me a full-time job chopping weed for "lip baggies" (sandwich bags of pot). He demonstrated proper chopping techniques while I rested on the countertop, my short legs dangling from the bar. At his command, I twisted my body to cup my left hand inside his right palm. He wrapped my tiny digits over the razor blade with care, then moved our limbs together, swooping up and down over dollhouse trees.

Dad taught me how to separate seeds and stems from the good bud, and we filled the lips three fingers deep. He emptied tiny brown boxes of JOB cigarette papers by the dozen and sprinkled in my finely chopped dope like a chef finishing off a gourmet dish.

King could roll and spit-seal joints faster than I could slurp chocolate milk. Those small doses of loose weed and pre-rolls were necessary in order for us to sell and move kilos, bricks, and bales in bulk. They were insurance: a sample for a would-be client or a venal treat for a narc's silence.

"Kids make the best hustlers," King told me the week after I was expelled from preschool. He lifted me onto the counter and coated his arms with palmfuls of petroleum jelly from the biggest Vaseline tubs Walmart sold. Then he greased up mine.

"No one expects a runt in a *Looney Tunes* T-shirt to shank you," he explained.

"Budgie!" he said and pointed to my chest, then sealed my street name with a Vaseline cross to my forehead.

"Budgie," I parroted, finger to my own chest.

I was thirty-six when I learned that a budgie is a parakeet. They are as skilled at call-and-response as larger parrots, perfectly mimicking their owner's vocabulary and syntax.

At age four, if I was going to help him sling drugs, he needed me to, first, be his canary in the coal mine and, second, copy his every move.

"Guns are for idiots," he added. "Here." He handed me my first pocketknife, a foldout two-inch blade with a horse and buggy painted on the handle. Knives teach you to accept the inevitable. "You'll get stabbed," he said, "but you'll survive. No big deal."

Besides, that's what the Vaseline was for. An enemy's grip, punches, and knife points would slip right off. I'd be ready.

He pumped his shiny green-bean arms to demonstrate a frenzy of imaginary switchblade thrusts to the liver.

"You try," he said.

I willed my spaghetti arms to slice the air.

"Ten-hut! Where is your post, soldier?" he asked, saluting me.

"Back wall, sir!" I said.

"Ten-hut! What is your duty, soldier?" he asked.

"Look around, sir!" I answered.

"Everyone is your enemy, soldier," he said, his constant twitch making his heavy overalls move in jerks like the ancient Ferris wheel at the Vermillion County fair.

Then he yelled out more questions. "Ten-hut! What's your assignment, solder?"

"Stranger danger! Explode, sir!" I said.

"Ten-hut! What do you say, soldier?"

"You can't fix crazy, sir!"

"At ease," he finished, leaving me to apply more Vaseline to my appendages while he wrapped a garbage bag around an armful of marijuana bricks and took it out to the trunk.

A minute later, King burst through the trailer door, back from dropping off the bricks, his hazel eyes nearly hidden under the brim of his dirty Yankees cap. "I'm going to *get* you, little girl!" he growled in a monster voice, grabbing me by the arm.

I jerked myself free, leaped off the counter, and forced my slimy limbs into a fighting stance. "I'll *kill* you, fucking dickhead!" I screamed, holding an imaginary knife to his gut because I'd been too flustered to draw the real one he'd just given me.

Insanity was the best defense, King said. No one—not a kingpin, cop, dealer, enemy, or shrink—wanted wild on their hands. In King's book, the unexpected explosion of a preschool dropout with a knife would pay for itself in dividends.

"At ease," King said. "Good job, Budgie." He patted me on the head. My jagged bowl cut bounced.

Weeks before I'd been expelled, King had cut my hair at home with paper scissors as punishment for yet another preschool crime. As my wavy brown locks fell to the floor, he told me to toughen up.

"Pain is the brain killer," King said.

"Pain is the brain killer," I parroted.

Before my preschool expulsion, I'd been a joyful kid with long dark tresses that were wild like me. My flowing unkempt hair had been the only part of preschool me that signaled carefree. As a ratty-looking kid whose napping blanket was an old green towel, I savored anything that made me feel like I belonged. And I was a little ham from the moment I learned to ride a seesaw. The first toddler at Valley Preschool to wake up an entire gang of napping rug rats, I then got them to gyrate their hips in the dark to a vocal solo of "The Heat Is On."

But I went too far for King when I lifted my dress and flashed my Strawberry Shortcake underwear to the boys on the playground. Chopping my hair off was my penance. Even though I inherited that showmanship from King, he was the first to put an end to it. If I were bold enough to flash boys for attention, I'd be bold enough to get him caught. After all, it was a knife-toting preschool drug lookout he needed, not an entertainer.

I asked King why he got to keep his black curls if I couldn't have mine. Except for his clean-shaven *Miami Vice* phase when he swam in cocaine and wore pastel shirts, he grew his curly beard down to his chest.

"It's sacred," he said, stroking what he referred to as his rabbinic coif.

"Thou shall not trim the corners of thy beard," King paraphrased Leviticus 19 in one of the Scripture lessons he taught me between knife-fighting sessions. He tapped his oily finger to his joint, ashing on the commandments.

His stained ball cap covered his friar's bald scalp. Only shoe-polish curls remained on the back and sides. He tied them back with rubber bands he stole from rich people's newspapers.

King's exposure therapy program continued the whole year I was four, a school designed to help me face our known or unknown enemies. It was built to replace childhood naïveté with the threat of evil realities. If innate responses to danger were fight, flight, or freeze, King wanted an explosion. The curriculum included studying the details of *Nightmare Theater*, a poor man's *Tales from the Crypt*. The host, Sammy Terry ("cemetery"), was a ghoulish Hoosier who wore yellow dish gloves and green contouring makeup. When Sammy wasn't on, King played me Vincent Price's voiceover at the end of Michael Jackson's "Thriller."

When out in the world, King moved with the same explosive mannerisms he expected of me. His manic, pinprick eyes and Vaseline-soaked skin were a warning to everyone: *If you cross me, my haymakers are going to shred you worse than a spring tornado.*

King's uncontrollable tendencies were what led his parents to enroll him in Culver Military Academy's eight-week summer program when he failed ninth-grade English. Culver assigned King to their famous cavalry. Dad slept in a tent and took care of the animals in the sweltering heat. By August he'd ridden a colonel's favorite horse to death "just for fun." When King told the story, he threw his head back and cackled, revealing his vampire-like incisors, mocking the colonel's frantic efforts to catch him. His peers hid him in the naval brigade until my grandparents came for him a few days later.

King escaped the colonel's kill order the summer he was

fourteen only to deal with the wrath of a hostile Vermillion County draft board in his twenties.

"Never face a kill room," King said. "Got it?" He wrapped his hand around my neck like a dog collar. "Better to die on the spot than to be stuffed in a sack." He shuddered when he said this, recalling the times he was tortured at a stateside military brig in a metal coffin called a hot box. Dad was a twenty-year-old troublemaking marine serving six months' active duty in California. It's clear the military thought him too wild. His officers held lighters to his feet week after week to coerce him into signing paperwork to volunteer for full-time service in Vietnam. But he never relented.

Still, the hot box broke him. His 1966 letters home became garbled. Illegible. Chaotic. To avoid the draft, he'd joined the reserves in Danville, Illinois, after flunking out of a Georgia college. In his fifth year as a military reservist, he went AWOL and was court-martialed. Marines his age were sent to arrest him, just like the Culver colonel had issued a kill order. But then, nothing.

"Nixon sent a letter. He freed me," King bragged to his disciples over our trailer counter stacked with drugs.

No one saw Nixon's pardon that allegedly freed King from his military duty. His military warrant just disappeared, along with his remaining mandatory service orders. Consequences evaporated and, with them, any self-calibration that could have come from weighing the risks. After that, King's confidence grew in miles; the severity of his schizophrenia did too.

That brand-new kitchen counter we scratched like a lotto ticket when I was four was tame compared with what was to come. By the time I was reading mildewed R. L. Stine mysteries in elementary school, the ceiling and floor of the Ninth Street trailer were completely razored to accommodate King's daily wiretap searches. When my father got so paranoid about the feds that he no longer used the front door, he sawed a manhole in the kitchen floor. He'd crawl in and out from underneath the metal skirting, the "trapdoor" covered with a recliner even the rats had abandoned. The king-sized mattress my parents had put on layaway when they bought the place was stripped to its coil bones to stave off federal bugs. Only a tissue paper's worth of pillow top remained, but the bands of cash taped to the water heater had multiplied.

Viper leveraged King's reputation for insanity (his diagnosed schizophrenia) and penchant for knives to sell and intimidate. King's history in Vermillion County—from his high school theatrics to running gangs to weaseling out of indictments to threatening to stab his own brother—made him Viper's prized calf. With King as his regional manager, Viper shuffled hay and blow.

My parents stored plastic-wrapped bricks and bales of drugs floor-to-ceiling behind the mirrored doors of their bedroom closet, which gave Viper a use for the Lady too. Her bedridden tendencies made her the watchdog we needed to guard the immense stash in the trailer's back bedroom. And I was the ace Viper hadn't expected: a parakeet lookout trained up in King's exposure therapy program.

During my first six years of life, we graduated from moving thousands of dollars of drugs in car trunks to tens and hundreds of thousands with trucks and trailers, dipping into and out of warehouses across the states. The bonus was built-in money laundering: Kiddie rides ran on America's spare quarters.

As the war on drugs ramped up, so did our defense against

it. Viper planned to move us out of the trailer and into a sprawling farmhouse where we could hold a grain elevator's worth of contraband. But we never made it that far. Though King and the Lady both held college degrees, they weren't business savvy. My parents were the kind of folks who got wild hares of ideas, like picking up and moving cross-country to follow a TV preacher and have a baby at age forty-one. Or starting a mail-order scheme that exchanged dollars for advice people could get for free.

Three Easters before I was born, King and the Lady met at the Rollman Psychiatric Institute in Cincinnati, Ohio. Mom had settled in Cincinnati in the late 1950s, when she and her first husband moved for his work. King arrived in Ohio by way of the beaten path: hitchhiking and wanderlust. For him, Cincinnati was far enough away from Vermillion County to start fresh but close enough to ricochet back.

The Lady had one son from her first marriage. She was satisfied with an only child. But King was adamant. He wanted a *daughter*—immediately. My parents were married by Christmas and wanted to be pregnant by Epiphany. When that failed, they stacked the deck with a church doctor and a medical doctor who told them they needed faith and warmer weather. A visit to Dr. Robert Schuller, a midwestern preacher who led a successful TV ministry from the Crystal Cathedral, happened to supply both. Dr. Schuller's positive-psychology self-empowerment sermons were an update from the 1940s and '50s Christianity that King and the Lady had been raised on. He was old-school enough to be familiar and just edgy enough to not be their parents' religion. They packed a U-Haul and headed to L.A. to sit at his feet. On the way, they saw a rainbow in the desert and knew I was in the cards.

When I was born, King and the Lady called me "Rainbow Girl" as a sign of the covenant between Noah and God, because I was a healthy baby born to a geriatric forty-one-year-old mother, a near miracle during the Carter era. "Tough times never last . . . but tough people do!" they said in unison each time they told my birth narrative.

Dr. Schuller was a Sunday staple for my parents, even though they'd gone broke in California three months after I was born, prosperity gospel running dry.

Pious men in shiny suits were always shaking leather Bibles at us through one of our three TVs in the trailer. The Lady had been raised on Billy Graham's southern tent revivals and claimed to be pious (she was not). King claimed to be Jewish (he was not). The only certainty I had about faith was that it was Dr. Schuller who had led them to me.

But faith doesn't fill a refrigerator.

After coasting back to Indiana on borrowed gas money, they settled in Vermillion County. Odd jobs followed, as did resignations and firings. Fancy college degrees couldn't mask mental illnesses.

Viper and Carnival Captivations was an easy fix. Viper had the brains to move inventory through America's arteries, funneling it to us to distribute in our region. But the trafficking risks grew, even as Americans' insatiable vice appetite did too.

Besides, my father preferred trunk jobs for a couple of bands of cash. Our trailer was just fine for us. We were poor people with poor ways; home was the path of least resistance.

TWO

My First Drug Drop

WHEN KING DISMISSED ME FROM MY WEED-CUTTING shift or when I felt artsy from catching his congregation's exhales, I retreated to my bedroom off the shotgun hall. Even as a preschooler, I was set up with my very own TV and cable box. I sat at a card table—my worktable—and painted construction paper with old nail polish to MTV music videos, drinking Hawaiian Punch from a tall can.

The Lady didn't cook, and we couldn't afford lunch meat, so I ate ketchup sandwiches until my mouth broke out in ulcers, a condition I dealt with well into my high school days. When drug trafficking picked up, we bought bologna and ate it alongside scrambled eggs with cheese. The first time I ate real mashed potatoes at a cafeteria, I let each salty, buttery bite pool on my tongue until it disintegrated into mealy mush. It was so unbelievably good.

Before bed each night, I lowered myself into the plastic garden tub in the corner of the trailer's only bathroom. My parents used the three-by-three-foot standing shower, but I wanted to soak myself in my own hot pool of Joy dish soap bubbles. I swam until I was pruned. The skunk smell of the day melted away like the make-believe "mashed potato" bubbles I scooped onto plastic doll plates. My daydream meals poured over the sides like lava. That bathtub was my own womb of warmth and cleanliness, a place where I could play like a child. It was my safe space.

Finally, the day came when King announced that I had graduated from his exposure therapy program and I was ready for my first drug drop.

The night it was to happen, I went in to see the Lady before we headed out. "Bye, Mom," I said. I stood on my tippy-toes to catch a glimpse of her head propped up on a pillow in the direct line of shotgun-house fire. She flipped her wrist at me like she was shooing a cockroach, her TV blaring gospel hymns. When I approached her for a goodbye hug, she peered at me through glasses as thick as basement block windows. I busied myself with helping her: straightening her cardboard nightstand cluttered with Afrin nose spray, tissues, a lamp, and a sticky glass of ginger ale. When I tried to get her attention by mimicking spraying Afrin in my nose, the Lady said it wasn't for kids but was something folks coming off the booger sugar had to contend with.

"I've never seen anyone make a nest like your mother," King said from the hallway, shaking his head. He tossed her a lip baggie while he waited on me to say goodbye. She didn't seem to hear him.

King had spent the day shuffling inventory into the crimson Oldsmobile we called "Big Red" like the chewing gum, so it was ready to go when we headed out. The car was "a boat of a girl," my parents would say, having eyed her for a trunk that could fit a small church choir. Big Red was fancy with whitewall tires my parents said were "as foolish as a fat cat's cravat!" King preferred gray cars. But he said this one had dropped in his lap. The Lady used to say that if Big Red could talk, she'd put us all *under* the jail. King corrected her, saying that Big Red kept us under the protection of our Lord.

When we slid into Big Red that night, King placed his index and middle fingers on the dashboard crucifix he super-glued to every vehicle he drove, whether he owned the car or not. He muttered, "Bless, bless, bless" and "Precious Jesus!" and slammed the driver's door. Clumps of cherry air fresheners in the shape of trees swung from the rearview mirror, and I snuggled up next to him on the velveteen armrest we called "the hump." His overalls smelled like Old Spice, marijuana skunk, and Vaseline.

King steered out of the gravel driveway like the wheel was made of hot iron. He left the radio and car lighter to me. From the hump, I leaned forward and dialed the knobs, then pressed the lighter in for him.

"We're on a tight schedule," he said through clenched teeth, mimicking the lockjaw accent we heard on TV from rich people who donned silk neck scarves. King didn't trust anyone who didn't keep a snotty Walmart bandana in their greasy pocket.

"Let's hit the Dairy Queen on the way home, Budge!" King said, Big Red bouncing over the crumbled blacktop. Ice cream was the treat my father promised after all successful endeavors. Most days, my tummy rumbled like a dryer with shoes in it, so I could already taste the chocolate malt.

"You got your knife?" he asked.

I tapped my dirty cutoffs as the last sliver of light vanished over the cornfields. Big Red rolled down Ninth Street and out onto the highway, past the Walmart. The Dairy Queen was in the other direction.

King held the last inch of his paper-rolled joint between needle-nose pliers, waiting for a flame. The car lighter popped, and I pulled it out, coils glowing like fiery ringworm.

"Take the wheel, Budge," he said, lighting his joint.

I mimicked his light hold while he savored the last of his weed.

"Drive in the middle of the road—nothing's coming."

It was new-moon dark by the time we hit the rural route. We weren't city folk, but I wanted the familiar potholes closer to home. King always said people did desperate things in the dark. My four-year-old heart pounded faster than my father's radar Fuzzbuster beeped when passing a roadside cop.

If everyone was my enemy, I wanted the doughy arms of my mother, who, on occasion, would squeeze me into the crook of her arm like a sleeping infant if I seemed especially pitiful. With her stringy gray hair fanned out on a striped pillow, she let me watch Pat Robertson or Johnny Carson with her. But fretting for her company in the presence of my father was unsettling. Even as a little kid, I knew that thinking of the Lady as my safety blanket was desperate. I already understood that my job was to anticipate and meet her needs. And in our drug-trafficking crime family, the Lady's catatonic dependence was more dangerous than King's viciousness. The former would get you killed, Dad said.

I didn't want to distrust King's expertise on this first big drop. But he was driving me on unknown dusty roads to a house deep in the sycamores that I could identify only by the warm light coming from the windows as we drove up.

When we pulled into their drive, I could tell it wasn't trailer-park living. They had rich people's real glass windows that looked onto a sturdy dining room table. When we walked in, the scent of a home-cooked meal lingered, a smell I knew only in my grandmother's kitchen. My grandparents lived twenty minutes away in Dana. They made family dinners so filling I rolled off their rickety wooden chairs. On holidays and birthdays, I drooled over Grandmother's Chef Boyardee box pasta doctored up with ketchup and brown sugar. A meal like that stayed with you for days.

The door opened, and we were greeted by a tall man with a head full of salt-and-pepper waves and a Sam Elliott mustache. The tattered red cutoff shirt he wore told me his veined biceps would beat me in hand-to-hand combat. When he smiled and shook my father's hand, his nicotine-stained teeth were so spread out in his mouth it looked like God had forgotten to give him a full set. He seemed nice enough. But the woods and quiet were how you got yourself to a kill room. King and Sammy Terry taught me that.

I waited for King's signal. If he liked someone, he called them "good buddy." If he was suspicious, he had his blade against their belly before they could blink, promising to gut them like a pig. King's judgment was ruthless; once, he'd vowed to fillet his youngest brother at my grandmother's supper table.

But it was all "good buddies" this night.

I followed King into the living room. In tandem, we sank deep into soft leather couches. With his signature twitches and jerks, King stopped talking only long enough to hawk a smoker's loogie into his snotty bandana. He wiped the spit from his vampire teeth. As trained, I fumbled with the strings on my cutoffs, scanning the room for threats. Taxidermied deer heads were poised on walls, and the doorways were covered by army blankets, which wasn't unusual for Indiana, where folks cut off square footage in the name of conditioned air. But what caught my eye was a stuffed wildcat at the top of the stairs behind the dealer.

The man interrupted my trance. "What do you think of *that*?" he asked, nodding toward the stairs. I turned red, failing my first lookout.

"Budgie loves cats!" King said, slapping me on the knee and disclosing more information about me than I'd wanted.

"Go check it out," the man said, like a warm uncle.

"No," I said dead-faced, thinking, *I will kill you, dickhead.*

"It ain't gonna bite you," he added, lighting a joint.

"Run and play with that good tiger, Budge," King said.

I slumped off the sofa and took the carpeted stairs up to my mark, pouty and betrayed. I resented being trained in looking out and hotheaded knife fighting only to be relegated to entertaining myself with a glassy-eyed feline.

My "ten-huts!" were wasted; I was a soldier who had lost her post. But when I sat next to the stuffed cat, a thought hit me: *Is King being strategic? The top of the stairs gives me a better view.* I could watch the men and the door. Back on duty, I clenched my jaw so hard I thought I'd break my baby teeth. On the landing, I palmed the carriage knife in my pocket and sat tall, ready to call out "Stranger danger!" and stab someone in the privates. I wouldn't go down without an explosion. But in these backwoods, a gunshot would go unnoticed, as would a trailer-park preschooler. The insanity that might be enough for someone in town to say, "Thanks, but no thanks, kid," would be wasted here in the silent forest. We were already as dead as furry mammals on pedestals.

But no one came to kill King.

No one came to push me to my death.

I feigned interest in the creepy cat while King talked, the client unable to get a word in edgewise. King could sell you shit-on-lettuce. Nobody wants to watch someone eat a shit sandwich. King and the man finally got up to go outside, where I'm certain King transferred goods for cash, then came back in laughing.

They shook hands, and King called for me. "Time to go, Budge!"

"Nice meeting yous," the man said, his mouth stretched into a wide grin under his walrus mustache.

I frowned in return.

When Big Red finally cranked to take us home, I whispered, "Precious Jesus," like I'd heard King and Tammy Faye Bakker say.

"Sorry, Budge. Dairy Queen's closed," King said, patting me on the head. "I'll make it up to you."

I was already too sad to care. My lookout and knife training had been wasted on Sam Elliott. I hadn't helped; no one needed me. "It's okay," I said, not wanting King to know I was upset. I slid over into the passenger seat from the hump and twisted myself small into the collapse of exerted energy.

Looking back, I realize I was a parental child who longed to take care of King and the Lady. Expressing my own needs and emotions was a risk I was never willing to take. It could lead to abandonment. And I needed King to need me to keep a lookout, explode in a knife fight, or curse somebody out. I needed the Lady to need me as her bedside maid and listening ear. If neither of them needed me, I wouldn't be of value. My worth was tied to my helpfulness.

"But you did good," he said, sensing my disappointment.

My tummy rumbled. I wondered what the mustache man had been eating off that big table.

We were still in the woods, driving down a gravel road, when King said, "Budge, pop me a li—"

King's arm was in midair when the deer hit the glass. Its sprawled legs gnarled our grill before it rolled onto the hood and shattered the window. My head was already ducked to start King's light, so I hit the radio face first and tumbled forward onto the floorboard.

The engine ran; King never braked. We didn't even pull over.

"You all right?" King asked, offering a hand to pull me up from the dirty carpet.

"Yes, sir," I said.

"Deer got us," he said, the headlights glowing down the dirt road in front of us, no animal in sight. My cheek was on fire, and I patted the side of my face to make sure the skin was still attached. The smell of burnt deer fur seeped in through the car vents, and I was certain that flames would lick up from the hood any second.

King hadn't stopped to inspect the car like I'd seen the dads on TV do. He was calm as he squinted through the shattered window. With bands of cash in the trunk and some drugs still on us, he had to be. My father steered back into the middle of the road, busted grill burning with deer guts.

King taught me that if something or someone is coming straight for you—a person, a car, a deer, anything—you hit the literal or metaphorical gas.

"Knock it right out of the way," he said, swishing his arms like he was fanning a campfire. King moved through the world like this—with a hubris that defied physics.

I could barely breathe.

"Lucky," he said after we inched back into town unnoticed and pulled into the trailer's drive.

By the time King parked and shut off the engine, Big Red was smoking. I walked to the front of the car and stared, transfixed by the gore I saw in the lone light of our kitchen window. Brown and white hair stuck to the radiator; deer blood had turned into crispy scabs and smelled like plastic left on the Lady's forgotten curling iron.

I was certain the fiery death that had missed us on the back road would come for us here. King taught me not to be afraid of stone-eyed men or even the cops. But the natural order of things—cause and effect—terrified me.

"Let's go, Budge," King commanded, holding the trailer door open for me.

At that moment, it wasn't the trauma of training or belonging to a drug-trafficking crime family or kill rooms or even prison that terrified me. It was the overconfidence of a delusional, schizophrenic man who'd outrun horse murder, the Culver colonel, hot-box torture, a court-martial, Vietnam, and drug indictments. It was my father's indifference to how close we'd come to death, which had appeared to us on a moonless night in the form of a deer sent to kick us from the slumber of believing we were invincible.

I dragged my feet in the gravel and didn't want to go inside. What if the car exploded and caught the trailer on fire while we slept? What if the deer had died a slow, painful death and its relatives sought revenge? Since we'd been at the drop house full of preserved animals, a campaign against us didn't seem farfetched.

But the unexpected smell of blueberry muffins hit me as I walked up the rusted metal steps to the trailer door King held open. My anger at the wasted night, my disappointment at no Dairy Queen, and my fear of Big Red turning into a bomb evaporated with the promise of baked goods.

Once a year, the Lady bought muffin mix at the discount grocery store and set it on the counter like a carrot, with the deal that if I were good, she'd fix them. Days would pass, and I would be on my best waitress behavior, attentive to her every need.

"When you making muffins?" I'd ask.

"My get-up-and-go done got up and went!" she said too many times to count, laying her greasy head on the pillow.

Maybe tonight she'd sensed that we'd worked hard and I'd had no chocolate malt. I hoped she knew intuitively that a deer had totaled Big Red and we'd nearly died. Or that I'd been forced to stare at a stuffed cat for hours. Maternal instincts activated, maybe she'd felt sorry for us for dealing late at night in the woods and coming home to ketchup sandwiches.

The light above the stove was on. It always was at night, which made the house feel warm. But there were no hot muffins resting on the burners, fresh from the oven. *Has the Lady taken them to her room?*

The hall was dark, and I pressed my palms to the panels on each side to feel my way to the back bedroom.

The door was cracked. The Lady was in bed, watching Carson.

"I smell blueberry muffins, and I—" I said, about to politely ask for one, when something on her cardboard nightstand caught my eye. The lamp sitting on top of it was smoking, a baby flame dancing its way up to the ceiling.

"You're on fire!" I screamed and pointed.

"What?" she said, lifting her chin.

"Fire!" I yelled.

The Lady had draped a gray sweatshirt with a blue sailboat over the lamp for ambience.

King heard me, ran to the back, and pushed me to safety. He threw the smoking shirt to the ground and stomped it out. It melted the nylon fibers of the cheap carpet, and the room filled with the smell of burnt plastic.

The Lady finally sat up, looking confused behind her Coke-bottle glasses. "That was my favorite shirt, you no-good son of a bitch," she said.

"Goddammit, Judy, you were going to burn the place down!"

"Well, it's so bright in here!" she said.

"Why the hell do you have the light on? You're watching TV! You could've leveled us to the ground!" he said, arms outstretched toward the closet.

By "us," he meant the inventory, the trailer, and her, in that order.

"Oh, calm down, Rick. You're being *psychotic*!" she said.

"Me and Dana's been out working, and here you been laying on your fat ass!"

"Working? Working! You never worked a day in your life!"

I backed out of the room and slunk down the hall to my own room, tummy rumbling.

They continued to yell.

Smoke, fear, sadness, and anticipation yielded to grief. The smell of burnt deer and nylon stayed trapped in my nose.

I never did get those blueberry muffins. Instead, I skipped my Joy bubble bath and put on my Care Bear pajamas. The volume on my MTV music videos muffled their fight, and I sat at my worktable and painted on construction paper.

Later, a knock on the trailer door grew louder when no one came out to answer it.

My heart raced, and my jaw snapped shut like the mousetraps in our kitchen. The training I hadn't used at tonight's drop would prove effective now. I'd have a chance to impress King so he'd trust me on the next drop, instead of relegating me to babysitting mounted pets. I grabbed my knife and left my room, the dirty carpet gritty underneath my bare feet. I pulled a kitchen stool to the door to look through the peephole.

It was Viper with a black trash bag in his arms.

"Hey, kiddo!" he said when I opened the door. "Got something for you."

Viper was well dressed in name-brand clothes and smelled like how I imagined movie stars did. His sandy hair was graying and fluffed, like he'd just tugged it away from hot rollers. Tall and slender yet solid as an oak, Viper was the kind of man who took up space but didn't threaten you with his stance. Instead, the only hint at his hatchet history was a jagged line that sliced his cheek crosswise and dimpled when he talked. Viper lived far away, but it was no surprise when he or King's entourage showed up at the trailer late like this— they always did minutes after King yelled "Talk to me!" into our beat-up phone. These were good buddies my father trusted with his life—and mine. He called them my uncles. Some of them called the Ninth Street trailer a party house. They lounged in the living room at King's feet as he prophesied, inhaling his stories and smoking his drugs. When they came over, I skipped around the room, trying to catch their clouds in my mouth. When I was older and some of them disappeared, King told me they'd joined the circus. They'd gone to "college," he clarified years later, our family's euphemism for prison. But tonight, no one had yelled "Talk to me!" into our phone.

"Here you go," Viper said. He pulled a brand-new My

Little Pony sleeping bag from the garbage bag. His eyes shined and he smiled so big the line on his face caved into folds.

"Take it to your room and try it out!" He balled up the bag and tucked it under his arm. Then he guided me by my shoulders back to my room.

Like my grandparents, Viper was always doing this kind of thing: bringing me toys and clothes. He lived in a rich person's house off a rural route in the middle of nowhere, not even in Vermillion County. By flyover standards, he was wealthy, boasting a full carpeted basement and cars with legal tags you didn't have to switch around and ignitions you didn't have to start with a screwdriver. If I'd ever gotten one, I would have put a tooth fairy's quarter on the fact that Viper was smart. It took wits to motivate my languid parents to move kilos and bales in kiddie-ride carcasses across state lines with only King's recklessness to protect us. Viper had a lot of faith—or desperation—to deal with the likes of us.

He stood at the door of my room and smiled. I flattened the sleeping bag onto my dirty floor and squirmed inside, fluff up to my chin.

"You stay right here while I go talk to your dad," he said, leaving the door open a crack.

I heard the three of them murmuring for a few minutes, and I knew Viper would take care of the fight, the fire, and Big Red. He always did. Then he walked back down the hallway, the black garbage bag covering a rigid object in his hand. He whispered good night as he walked by my room, and then he closed the trailer door. I fell asleep in the My Little Pony cocoon.

The next morning, I shuffled to the living room, rubbing my eyes. The sun was up, bright through the closed curtains. King was gone.

I visited the Lady, still in bed.

"Your dad was going to kill us!" she announced.

I showed her the sleeping bag.

"That's nice," she said dismissively.

"Your father is *psychotic*," she continued. It rolled off her tongue with a staccato sharpness as piercing as King's hazel eyes. "Psy-cho-tic!"

"Where's Dad?" I asked. I didn't know if psychotic was a place. King usually got me up in the mornings with chocolate milk.

"Thanks to me, Viper came and got that *terrible* gun last night. He came because *I* called him and asked him to," she bragged.

"You're alive thanks to me," she added. "He's psychotic, I'm telling you."

You can't fix crazy, King taught me. He should know. He'd met my mom, after all, on a psych ward.

The real danger of my drug-trafficking childhood wasn't the razor blades in my toddler hands or the knife training or the kiddie-ride business or even the drug drops on lonely back roads.

The real danger was living in the single-wide trailer with King and the Lady.

The real threat was home.

THREE

Lewman Crazy

CRAZY, IT TURNS OUT, COMES IN ALL FORMS. INSANITY is a kind of repetitive, insidious brutality as heart-breaking as adults reenacting their own psychiatric confinements in a trailer full of drugs. My parents were never able to break free of it. For my father, his madness started at home with his own parents: the *Lewman* way.

"Budge, the only difference between us and them is who's got the keys," King said cryptically when he returned to the trailer the day after the deer wreck. He never mentioned why he'd left, the Lady's fire, their fight, Viper coming and taking the gun, or even Big Red.

That morning we sat at the kitchen counter, and King lifted me to sit on top, my legs dangling over the edge. We razored drugs into submission together, like nothing had happened.

"Odd man out, your mom and me," King continued, tipping his Yankees hat toward the back bedroom, where the

Lady was napping. It was a rare moment of showing tenderness for her, even though she'd just called him psychotic.

"Takes one to know one, I guess." He shrugged and took a toke of a freshly rolled joint.

King told me the story of the first time he'd seen the Lady on a psych ward at the Rollman Psychiatric Institute in Cincinnati, Ohio, early 1978. She was thirty-eight, freshly divorced, and beauty-queen thin. Her curly auburn hair still smelled like a perm. King was thirty-one, dapper in a horseshoe mustache and newly broken up with a Wiccan who'd given him genital warts. At that time, they were working at Rollman: King was a recreational therapist who played games for a living; the Lady was a psychiatric nurse who doled out (legal) drugs for her paycheck.

When their Rollman patients and colleagues found out Rick and Judy were engaged, they were unanimous in their belief that this match was too volatile to have a good ending.

King and the Lady had, in effect, written their own Kubrick characters: him, a draft-dodging, lawbreaking marine who used witness intimidation to facilitate his acquittal; and her, an entitled debutante who relished being taken care of inpatient and signed herself out with "Gone to the beach!" in cheerful cursive. In Hollywood terms, their combustion was certain. The success of their marriage was as guaranteed as a newspaper horoscope.

"Who's got 'em now?" I asked about the keys, swinging my legs from the counter, confused by King's initial metaphor.

While I picked seeds out of my cut pile, King reached into the kitchen cabinet he called his office and pulled out a dingy set of antique-looking keys on a stretched rubber band. "I do!" He jingled them and laughed. "This here's the keys to Rollman Inpatient Psychiatric Unit. Rick Lewman, certified recreational therapist, at your service," he added and saluted me.

"Check their pockets!" King shouted toward the back bedroom as the Lady watched TV.

In a rote call-and-response, she shouted back, "Draw up the Haldol!"

They cackled, and King jingled the keys again.

When King and the Lady worked at Rollman during those glory days in the late 1970s, they were on the other side of the keys as big-shot mental health professionals, back on locked wards, but as the staff who patients locked in.

That wasn't always the case. Between them, the 1960s brought accumulated diagnoses, criminal charges, and mental illness records as thick as phone books. For King, it had been schizophrenia, specifically schizoaffective disorder, which combined the worst symptoms of paranoid schizophrenia with depression and anxiety. The Culver horse murder, military prison (the brig), federal draft dodging, and a hefty Vermillion County grand jury indictment for drug distribution were all somewhat explained by his schizophrenia. For the Lady, it was narcissistic and dependent personality disorders, diagnosed in the 1960s after a handful of suicide attempts followed by inpatient lockups she fondly referred to as vacations.

"Beat-down dogs," King went on, referring to his own psych patients, while he unwrapped a brick of drugs. This was our family's term for anyone whom the world had subjugated. You could always count on King and the Lady to side with a beat-down dog, folks who were "capital-C crazy." Their empathy extended to anyone who had been rejected by their family or society. They raised me to be attuned to that sort of thing too. But for the Lady, the exception to the beat-down-dog compassion was always King's psychotic nature, which she said was as deft as the devil's. When the terror of his outbursts outweighed their usefulness in keeping away other criminals, she was vexed.

"I told 'em, 'Meet me back here at 6:00 A.M. *sharp*,'" he explained to me as we chopped, recalling a night in the seventies when he signed his wildest patients out for a major league baseball game. When he cranked the hospital van after the ninth inning, it sputtered like a deflating balloon. Anyone but King would have been terrified to be stranded with patients whose records were longer than the Mississippi River. But King liked to cut leashes. He turned his patients loose for a night of God-knows-what. Everyone went their separate ways, and everyone returned at sunrise. No one spoke of what kindnesses or misdeeds they'd done.

"You can't fix crazy," King said again, shaking out a handful of coarse marijuana under my razor blade.

He would know. He'd come by his own "you can't fix crazy" the hard way: a Vermillion County upbringing. "This place will make you feel alive even as it slits your throat." He drew a flattened hand across his neck.

That night, after our daylight loafing and storytelling, King itched to be in motion. Whether he was riding a bicycle or motorcycle or driving a car, truck, or hearse, King never sat still long.

"Time for a midnight bike ride, Budge!" he said, throwing a handful of joints into the front pocket of his overalls.

"I'll go get Mom," I said, excited for the outing.

King took a breath but didn't stop me.

"Who are you? Nurse Ratched?" the Lady said when I grabbed her arm and tried to peel her off the sweaty sheets. "I'm simply not outdoorsy." She pried her hand free of mine.

"We're staying close," I assured her.

"Close only counts in horseshoes and hand grenades!" She changed the channel on the TV.

"Oh, let her be," King yelled. He came for me down the hall, gripped my neck from behind like a shuffleboard stick, and steered me out the trailer door.

"You don't know how good you got it, kid. Your mom is happy right where she is."

He snapped his arm like he was delivering an invisible lashing and pretend-kicked my rear end, though he never did hit me. His own mother had delivered real whippings and kicks and beatings. She even kept a bullwhip on the living room wall. Thankfully the sins of the mother weren't visited on the granddaughter.

We locked the door, leaving the Lady in the trailer, and slid into the hot seats of a gray Cutlass, Big Red's replacement, just as the afternoon sun was fading.

Midnight bike rides always took place at Uncle Leuge's house in Dana. He was King's middle brother and also his oldest and best friend. They watched each other's backs and balanced each other out. While King wrecked everything he owned, Uncle Leuge kept pristine bikes of all shapes and sizes in his garage. King mooched off his brother's responsible nature, leveraging Leuge's desire to keep his own children (and niece) entertained. Midnight bike rides were King's favorite training ritual. They usually started as soon as the last frost had thawed, signaling that the never-ending gray Indiana winter had finally relinquished its grip.

"Midnight bike ride lesson number one: If you want to kill somebody, you do it in Vermillion County," King said and cackled.

"Precious Jesus!" He pressed his fingers to the crucifix

he'd just mounted to the dash. Then he tapped his overalls pocket full of joints.

Big Red's burnt grill was gone and, with it, my fear of being murdered by vengeful mammals.

I nestled into the seat, excited to head to Dana, where my two cousins would join our nighttime bike ride. King would imbue us three girls with curiosity about the surreal history of our land and people.

According to the atlas my paternal grandparents kept tucked into the back seat of their new minivan, Vermillion County was the Gumby of Indiana geography. With the Wabash River lining the east side of the county and no-good Illinois bordering us to the west, its land stretched so thin and long it nearly broke. King said summer was the perfect time to teach me lessons about home. My father was born in Vermillion County. He was the kind of wanderer who knew the value of home. No matter what any stranger or pundit said, to him Indiana was a magical place full of good buddies. Despite its dangers and dullness, it was familiar, he said, like a well-worn sweater that snugs you just right. King wanted me to have the security of home fitting like that.

In the car, King explained our county's layout. Our Ninth Street trailer in Clinton was in the southern third of Vermillion County. Dana sat due northwest, less than three miles from the Illinois border. Newport sat on the eastern side of the county and was home to the military's VX nerve agent plant.

Every summer, the Vermillion County fair was held in Cayuga, a stone's throw from that very plant. King and his brother Leuge attended the fair for its famous midnight peep shows, where schoolteachers would come clear from Indianapolis to strip for cash.

My father had never wanted to leave Dana. But the 1960s Vermillion County school consolidation began ripping Dana kids from their isolation. They were bused to Clinton, where they were spit on and called country scum. I learned early on that belonging to a place like Dana required a steel constitution.

"Why did you leave L.A.?" I asked him during one of our many geography lessons. It was a fair question. He and the Lady beamed on Sunday mornings as they watched *Hour of Power*, Dr. Schuller swaying on TV in a velveteen paneled robe like a winter nightgown.

"Lesson number two, kid: There's only so much sugar in the sack." King said this whenever he was out of drugs, time, or money.

"Besides, nothing's more hopeful than summer in western Indiana," he added. "Just look at this place, Budge." He motioned toward the lush cornstalks that lined Ninth Street across from our single wide.

"Your mom wanted to name you Renée," King said as we passed the abandoned Ninth Street playground in the gray Cutlass. "But I said, 'Hell no!'" He paused to light his joint and take a toke.

"This here's *Dana* from Dana, Indiana." He tapped my chest where my seatbelt would have been, had he not razored it out.

"Vermillion County is your birthright, Budge." He stretched his hands toward the corn, as if he were presenting gold bars. "Don't you let anyone tell you different."

I was oblivious to what it had taken for King to survive his earliest decades in Vermillion County. His violent upbringing at home and on the streets made my own terror management curriculum look cartoonish. But each summer, we did these bike tours and he reminded me. We rode without the heaviness of drugs or cash that needed to be hidden. It was a rare respite from slinging and the fetid trailer.

While the Lady complained about "the weather you can wear," King lived for these warm, dark nights.

"Nothing makes you feel richer than a full tank of gas," he said.

King thrived on motion. It didn't matter what kind. Driving, dropping, hitchhiking, train-hopping, bike-riding, or tripping. He was never still. Midnight bike rides calmed his jitters.

As we drove up Ninth Street at sunset, I watched the road pass under our feet through the holes in the floorboard. We coasted on siphoned fuel and bootleg Anita Baker jazz tapes toward the Clinton Dairy Queen, which sat on the bank of the Wabash River next to a chipped concrete four-seasons fountain. King was making amends for the reneged promise after the deer hit us last night. I eagerly accepted my stipend of a cold chocolate malt poured into a *Dennis the Menace* cup. We stood at the fountain, then walked over to a wooden grandstand looking out onto the Wabash River.

Every Labor Day weekend, thousands of Italians gathered here for the Little Italy Festival. They stomped grapes and guzzled wine and celebrated their immigrant ancestors who mined coal in Vermillion County.

"This here's where your great-grandmother Gramps pushed your great-grandfather off a homemade raft. See?" King said, pointing his greasy fingers beyond the Italian flags to sticks frozen in the muddy bank.

The Wabash River slices clear across Indiana like a butcher's hook. Its ominous current cuts across corn towns like ours until it unfurls into a welcome two-hundred-mile river wall between Indiana and Illinois. Just north of this watery border, it divides Vermillion from its neighbors. These waters keep violence in and outsiders out.

"Gramps didn't take shit from nobody," King said, nodding toward the water.

Gramps was King's paternal grandmother, a petulant-looking lady with cat glasses who scowled at me from black-and-white photographs.

"You say your prayers when you cross this river," he instructed, pointing up from the bank to the steel cage of a bridge.

King never did say how many people he knew in Vermillion County who had allegedly met watery deaths. My father's stories may have been stretched as long and thin as the county itself. But I knew for certain that our family had lowered concrete buckets into the river after midnight.

"Lesson number three: Natural elements make the best weapons," King continued, pointing to the bubbly flow of black water. "Let's go."

I slurped the last of the chocolate malt, and King let me shift the Cutlass in reverse as driving practice. He muttered, "What a no-good . . ." while I lit his joint and helped him steer. I knew he was talking about his own father. Gramps always reminded him of Richard. So did bridges.

My paternal grandfather, Richard Lewman, had been a World War II army captain in the Battle of the Bulge. One day while he was on winter bridge duty, blasting caps blew off the pinkie and ring finger of his left hand. Grandfather was honorably discharged with a Purple Heart and given a warm hospital bed in Kansas. That's where he met his future wife, Grandmother Dorothy, who was his nurse.

As King told it, Grandfather's blasting caps had been a

grenade. My father liked the drama of a pulled hand bomb. The truth was too ambiguous for him.

"He pulled that grenade on purpose!" King said, this time aloud and miming Grandfather's left hand. "The *two* fingers he didn't need on the hand he didn't use. Give me a goddamned break!"

We pulled out of Clinton onto Highway 63 north going toward Dana. The Renatto Inn, which everyone called "the Naughty Renaughty," sat right there off the highway, and as usual, the parking lot was brimming over with cars. It was the kind of roadside motel where you paid by the hour. The month I turned four, I'd even stayed there with King and the Lady, who packed our suitcases and inventory "for a vacation." I never knew if we were running toward something or away from it. But I taught myself how to shampoo my own hair in a Naughty Renaughty shower.

King's hand palmed the air outside the window as we hit eighty miles an hour on Highway 63. While the sun faded, I watched indigo skies coax endless miles of cornstalks heavenward. The wintry barren fields that had looked as heavy as corduroy months ago were forgotten like a bad harvest.

I understood King's love for this tough land when we took these highway rides at top speed, flashes of lush green stalks out the window calming me. Every time we made these drives, I felt like I was living a normal childhood, riding without the pressure of being a lookout.

But like everything else in King's crazy life, that tiny sliver of summer abundance and sanity was temporary. I was so charmed by the landscape, I forgot months of Indiana's infamous gray skies and unforgiving wind—and the destruction that comes from indoor boredom when you lived there.

"I have a veeshun," King announced just as we passed a sign for the turnoff to Ernie Pyle Elementary School.

Holding the inhale of his joint, he squeaked out the prophecy: "You shall have three sons, and you shall name them James, Joseph, and Joshua! You'll be a big-shot professor at ISU!" I didn't know what a professor was. But I knew Larry Bird had played for ISU (Indiana State University), and King had been a campus prophet there "back in the old days," he said. When he pressed his index and middle fingers to the crucifix and sealed his message with "Precious Jesus! Bless, bless, bless," I knew it had to be true.

"You got the book smarts, kid. And my Budgie ain't gonna be no beat-down dog."

I repeated his prophecy to myself.

As we pulled off Highway 63 onto 36, only the liminal moments of twilight remained. Dark was coming, and my heart raced a little, as if remembering the last time we were out last night.

We drove into Dana. The town is just over a quarter of a square mile of streets and alleys, landlocked by cornfields. There are no east-west roads into and out of town. The railroad and grain elevator anchor the south entrance; the ball diamond and old sewage trench sit at the north.

"This place used to be something else," King said, cutting the headlights as we drove through town. "Be on the lookout for Illinois plates," he whispered. "No-good, lazy SOBs."

In its heyday Dana had a thousand residents. A thriving railroad and a large grain elevator made the town a booming agricultural hub. People worked the fields and loaded railway cars to feed the nation. Civil War–era homes in pristine condition housed families with a basketball team's worth of kids.

My grandfather owned the town's busiest grocery store. An opera house, a theater, a broom factory, a laundromat, a bank, a garage, and churches all kept 1950s residents busy and faithful.

But prosperity is always temporary.

The glory days were gone, just like my parents' L.A. dreams. Caved roofs, broken windows, and vicious unleashed dogs anchored my own childhood.

It was pitch dark when we pulled into the blacktop driveway of the Lewman house in the middle of Dana, the very same house where King grew up with his parents and two younger brothers, Leuge and Boot. Our family calls it "the Lewman Museum" because it's one of the last houses in Dana without a tarp for a roof.

Leuge met us outside wearing an Indiana University shirt and ball cap. Tall, tanned, and confident, Leuge was the straight-edge middle child who took care of things. He was clean-shaven and fit, boating on the weekends at Raccoon Lake and maintaining a backyard above-ground pool. Leuge always squinted when he saw you, like he forgot who you were and really had to think about it. When he was satisfied enough that he knew you, he'd give you a warm hug and launch into a sordid Vermillion County story in his loud voice. His high-pitched laugh revealed vampire teeth identical to King's. I always felt safe around him.

Like King, Leuge had college degrees. The two brothers had even roomed together one year at ISU in the 1960s, back when boys wanted to carry books instead of guns in Nam. The year they lived together, King cemented his cult leader status, becoming a prophet who held secret meetings in the library stacks to overthrow the administration. Back then, King wore an olive-green corduroy suit, carried a briefcase, and drove a hearse. He was famous for wearing no under-wear and riding in the death mobile. Leuge tolerated his older brother's quirks.

The Lewman brothers earned undergraduate and gradu-ate degrees to avoid Vietnam. Leuge married a warm, tan, short-haired woman named Marietta, an Italian from Clin-ton. He taught public school until he got fed up with the low pay and mouthy parents. By the time I was born, Leuge was a big-shot insurance agent who'd landed some of the multi-million-dollar agricultural accounts in Vermillion County. People loved Leuge. They trusted him with their most valu-able assets: livelihoods steeped in black soil and the corn it yielded. He and my aunt Marietta had two blond-haired, brown-eyed girls: Lindah, who was five years older than me, and Doggy, who was six months younger.

Even as a kid, I got the sense that my uncle Leuge was dependable. He looked out for me like I was his third daugh-ter. It was Leuge who had kept King out of "college" (prison) for that hashish indictment that carried a twenty-year mini-mum sentence. While King was shooting up China white shipped to him from "the suckers who went to Nam" and sharing his hepatitis C, it was Leuge who had the wits to call a Bloomington lawyer, Lewellyn Pratt. Pratt got King acquit-ted on vagaries from the narc who'd allegedly seen the deal but was too dumb to provide specifics. It also didn't hurt that someone had tried to run the snitch off the road in Vermillion County. I never knew if it was King. Pratt got my father ac-quitted and told him, "Never call me again."

Had it not been for Leuge, King would have spent twenty years in prison and I wouldn't have been born. But like any brothers, they fought. Days before the indictment warrant was issued, King tried to kill Leuge. Years later when I asked my uncle what had happened, he just said, "Those were crazy times."

"Hey good buddy!" King greeted Leuge when we pulled into the drive. My cousins ran out of the house and hugged me.

"Don't get comfortable, girls; we've got business to do!" King called as we ran to my cousins' playroom, where Barbies poured out of pink plastic houses.

The playroom had originally been our grandparents' bedroom. Uncle Leuge and Aunt Marietta bought the two-story Civil War house from Richard and Dorothy just after their girls were born.

Our grandfather and grandmother moved to Dana and married in 1946. They purchased the 1864 tinderbox when Leuge was an infant and my father was three. Here, while adjusting to eight fingers and papering over World War II wounds with money, they raised three boys and whipped two. Boot, the baby, was his parents' "Dolly," a cherub of a child placed on an altar like an untouched porcelain knick-knack.

With beatings as regular as breathing, King and Leuge coped with violence by dishing it out in kind. While their parents slept, the brothers jumped from their upstairs windows to lead street scuffles and set fires. While their parents worked, they threw knives in classrooms and led basketball court brawls, practicing their sailor language.

One afternoon when they were teens, Grandmother got word that King and Leuge were pummeling a townie. She hid behind the front door of the Lewman Museum and waited for her sons. When they opened the door, fresh from their gang victory, their mother pounced. She thrashed them with her bullwhip. They covered their heads with bloody knuckles and shrank and begged. Her stored-up rage at being gossiped about fueled her blows. It's hard to know if she was embarrassed that her sons were bullies or jealous at being outdone. Either way, the advantage of her surprise conquered them. King and Leuge would later say it was the worst beating they ever got, the three of them tangled up in sweat and blood. But at the first sign of Grandmother's exhaustion, King loosed his collar from his mother's grasp and sacrificed Leuge. He crawled out the door and ran across the street, where he watched through the living room window as his brother got the remainder of the beating.

Home was never safe. But the boys seemed to understand Grandmother's wrath. "I never got a beating I didn't deserve," Leuge would say.

The taupe-sided Lewman Museum, which housed generations of our family, remains untouched. No wall or knick-knack has been moved. Haunted with our grandparents' violence, the stairs to the boys' bedroom still creak and thump like leather whips cracking skin.

"Girls, come in here. I want to show you something," King yelled from the kitchen at the center of the house, jolting us out of our play with dress-up clothes and Barbies. When we got there, Leuge, Aunt Marietta, and King were talking. We stood next to the table, and he pointed to the yellowed linoleum.

"Underground Railroad came through here," King said, motioning to a two-by-two brown metal grate in the floor next to the pantry. "You'll learn about that in school."

Lindah, a fourth grader at Ernie Pyle Elementary School, nodded.

Leuge looked suspicious.

Aunt Marietta went to the oven and pulled out a cake. Then she handed us plates loaded with Oreos and cheese crackers. She was always taking care of us. As I ate my snack, I pretended she was my mother.

The phone rang on the kitchen wall, interrupting my daydream and King's history lesson.

Marietta answered. "Hello. Lewmans'."

It was Grandmother, inviting us all over for brown cows, her specialty drink of ice cream and Coke.

After selling the Lewman Museum to Leuge and Marietta, she and Grandfather had lived outside town in a blue Sears modular on wide-open acreage. When they got too old to manage the farm and its house, Grandfather bought a row of barn-red studio apartments behind the bank, and they moved back into town. Eager to settle on Dana's Main Street for access to groceries and friends, they renovated their studio, adding Grandmother's sitting room with paneled walls, pink carpet, and a pullout sofa bed I slept on when I spent the night. In the evenings, they watched TV and read the newspaper in their tiny living room lined with Ethan Allen bookcases. Grandmother kept an immaculate and cozy home and insisted we girls use proper terms like *Grandmother* and *Grandfather*. So we shortened it to "G&GL" behind their backs.

The childhood violence King and Leuge suffered at the hands of G&GL didn't mesh with our view of them. "Cognitive dissonance," King called it. It didn't even seem possible that our grandparents had been bullwhip child-beaters. But the townspeople—even our grandparents' own peers— corroborated two things: the violence the boys endured and the violence they perpetrated.

Everyone in Dana knew everyone else's business. It wasn't easy to keep secrets in a place the size of a big city's mall.

Before we even got to Leuge's, someone had already phoned Grandmother to tell her that King and I had snuck into the north side of town.

King rolled his eyes. "Girls, your grandmother is a piece of work."

"Girls, your grandmother Dorothy is *different*," Leuge corrected. "She raised us to be *different*. Your dad is her greatest success story." He pointed to King. "The rules never applied to Rick."

"Yeah, but neither of you boys ever went to 'college,'" Marietta chimed in, shaking her head as she dipped toothpicks into the cake. "'Cause there are two kinds of crazy in this world—regular crazy and *Lewman* crazy. And nobody wants to deal with Lewman crazy."

"Idiots," Leuge said, interrupting the lesson on our genetic insanity to nod toward the TV they kept above the refrigerator. Any Leuge commentary always started out of nowhere, after he evaluated something with squinty eyes and suddenly decided to mention it. Now the news story was covering a convicted death-row inmate one county over south at the U.S.'s primary federal prison for the death penalty, just thirty minutes from Dana. But that crime hadn't taken place in Vermillion County.

Even though King had been threatened with a twenty-year sentence by the Vermillion County district attorney, our family had only ever seen anyone get six months in "college." The brothers' classmate who had murdered his wife with a beer bottle got as much as a teen we knew who had broken his girlfriend's neck. Half a year of "education" seemed to be what a life was worth in Vermillion County. Legend had it that the last capital-punishment conviction in the county was in the early 1800s over a stolen twenty-five-cent bar of soap. The perp was hanged in Newport and buried in Eugene, a township known for its haunted houses.

From nursing-home serial killers to men run over by snowplows, King and Leuge reiterated the dangers of Vermillion County and sprinkled their true crime stories with details of punched prostitutes and kidnappings. They recounted these horror stories in a tone as innocuous as the pranks kids play at Halloween.

But the thesis of each of their stories was clear: Constant chaos was the norm. They were never deterred by near misses like the deer that nearly killed me and King on that drug drop or King's attempt at killing Leuge. The Lewman boys had already spent a lifetime dodging trouble. They felt—and in some ways they were—invincible. King and Leuge were tethered to an unbelievable Vermillion County history they couldn't shake.

"If you want to murder someone, you do it in Vermillion County," Leuge said, repeating the first lesson King had taught me.

"They don't get you for stuff like that here, girls," he added.

For all its violence, our fathers insisted that Vermillion County was a magical place if you knew how to survive it.

The girls, Aunt Marietta, and I stood by the alleged entrance to the Underground Railroad with King and Leuge as they jumped from how well the Lakers were playing to how well they'd beaten their common childhood enemies. The brothers had no allegiance to linear plots. But Vermillion County tales always had a villain, a victim, and a lesson. One minute we were hooked on Leuge's dramatic reenactment of a bloody stabbing; the next we were back with the brothers under the canvas tents at the Vermillion County fair, hearing (again) how teachers stripped for summer cash.

"They'd come clear from Indianapolis to do nudie shows for them carnies," Leuge said, squinting at the TV. "We was under that good tent, see." He used his forearms to mimic a military crawl.

"We saw that good teacher go right up to Paddlefoot," Leuge explained, telling how one of the fair security guards got a lap dance.

"Oh, she bathed them glasses," Leuge said, now out of his chair and acting out with Aunt Marietta's potholders how the teacher took Paddlefoot's glasses and wiped them with her gusset.

Our faces blushed as red as a Strawberry Shortcake doll.

"Oh, foot!" Aunt Marietta said, snapping her dish towel for Uncle Leuge to quit.

"Every single carny working that fair revolted when they cut that peep show. It was a bloodbath."

His eyes got big as ping-pong balls for emphasis. "There again, it happened here in Vermillion County," he said and sat down.

A frenzy of loud meows interrupted the kitchen stories. We all ran through the playroom and poured out onto the front porch. Across the street, Gunman Dan's run-down Victorian was overgrown with weeds as tall as the teens who tried to loot it. A life-size skeleton still hung in the trees out front, a holdover from Halloween. Dan, who was nearly blind, had shot at his family but missed. The attempted murder had secured him a place on the long list of Vermillion County failed "students" who'd been denied years-long matriculation into hard-time prison. Since the incident, they'd moved on and the brigade of feral cats had taken over.

"Oh, he never went to '*college*,'" Leuge had explained to us girls.

He squinted his eyes at the cats.

King was itching to ride. "Okay, girls. Let's get to business. I'm going to teach you how to run this town," he said, dog-collaring me with a cuffed hand around my neck, steering me away from the cats. Leuge disappeared into the garage. We followed my father back to the shed to start the midnight bike ride.

But I really wanted nothing more than to duck back into Aunt Marietta's warm kitchen. My cousins lived a different life. There were no plastic-wrapped bricks of drugs in their closets or bands of cash taped to their water heater. Marietta was always dressed and out of bed, shuttling them to school and dances and playdates. She washed and dried a load of laundry each day and kept a house that made you feel like you belonged. There were always snacks in her cabinets and food in her refrigerator.

"I love you like you're one of my own," she'd say. "I've got *three* girls, not two."

I wanted to listen to the hum of her dryer and play Barbies while the smell of cake wafted through the house. I looked down at the new white canvas Keds Aunt Marietta had just bought me. I didn't want to scuff them on a bike ride where King would teach us how to kick rabid dogs and out-wit cops. But my cousins loved midnight bike rides.

It was a signature King training they wouldn't get from Leuge. While my uncle forbade King from teaching Lindah and Doggy about the drug trade, he saw no harm in my father instilling street smarts we could all use inside the county lines.

Succumbing to the peer pressure of the group, I joined

King in the shed, where a bullwhip hung under a wooden sign that read, "LEWMANS."

"This is it, girls! Yah! Yah!" King said, taking the whip down and play-beating us. Our fathers never hid their parents' abusive tendencies. I suspect now the brothers' openness was about awareness and accountability. Secrecy fuels shame and generational cycles. Our knowledge of our grandparents' ferocity was a warning. We were to report even the slightest slap to King or Leuge. Even though their scars were decades old, we girls could still feel the heaviness of a Lewman childhood steeped in violence.

"I never got a beating I didn't deserve," Leuge reminded us.

King was less forgiving.

Our grandparents' tenderness toward us must have been an unspoken contract with King and Leuge. Physical violence against me, Lindah, and Doggy would have resulted in G&GL's slow, brutal deaths. And by the time they were fathers, the two brothers had the Vermillion County social capital to follow through on the threat.

I realize now that King's resentment toward his parents stemmed not only from the incessant physical abuse he endured but also from their lack of empathy for his schizophrenia. When he had his break (likely during those teen years), whips and military reform school weren't the "cure" he—or any child—needed. But times were different.

We grabbed bikes and prepared for this ritual. King was animated as he shared the best part of his childhood with us—one that happened mostly in the dark.

Different from knife lessons and razoring drugs for Dad and drops, King's midnight bike rides were focused on conquering everyday Indiana enemies: unleashed dogs, aggressive boys, methed-out men, drivers with Illinois plates, and demons.

"Wait here, girls," King instructed, inching Leuge's ten-speed out of the shed and into the alley. His stringy overalls hung over holey Walmart tennis shoes.

"Coast is clear," he whispered, ushering us out to join him.

We rolled out and around the corner to the front of the Lewman Museum. A gun barrel emerged from the garage, catching the shine of a streetlamp. Staccato pops followed. We could barely distinguish him in the dark, but it was Leuge, shooting BB gun pellets at Gunman Dan's cats.

King led us toward a tree in the front yard as Leuge fired his last round. Cats scattered. The meows quieted.

"This is where we hung that good Tiger," he said, motioning toward the tallest branches of the maple as it shifted in the hot summer wind. We straddled our bikes while King explained how he'd hung the family's cocker spaniel from a noose. Tiger was more fortunate than the colonel's horse. My father cut the rope just before Tiger died.

"Oh, he was all right," King dismissed our concern. We stared up at the tree as sulfur smoke lingered.

"It was Booty-Boy who killed him, girls," King said, reminding us of the first enemy he had: their baby brother, Boot.

"You remember that, girls. Your uncle Boot is a no-good," King said. "I should have killed him when I had the chance."

My father had held a knife to Boot's fat gut when Grandmother made the mistake of seating them together on Thanksgiving.

Our fathers' warning about Boot made him a monster in our books. We sided with our fathers. Besides, we had formed our childhood judgment about him quickly when we saw firsthand the way Boot neglected his own horses.

But when they were boys, Boot had let Tiger follow him a few blocks to Grandfather's Regal Grocery Store on Dana's Main Street, where the dog was run over by a car. Leuge scooped Tiger's body into a box and held vigil for him.

"Midnight bike ride lesson number four: Never trust a liar.

"This way!" King said, waving us on toward Main Street and retracing Tiger's last steps. As we rode, King repeated to Lindah and Doggy the first three lessons I'd gotten on the ride up to Dana from Clinton. "Lesson number one." The three of us chimed in; we knew this one by heart: "If you want to kill somebody, you do it in Vermillion County," we said in chorus.

"Lesson number two: There's only so much sugar in the sack, girls. You pick your fights carefully. Next, natural elements make the best weapons—right here's proof of that." King stopped suddenly at a dark alley on the way to Main Street.

"Eleven Baytons and one toothbrush," he said and entered the alley. "They weren't allowed out of the yard except on Saturdays when Rachel and Doughton Bayton went to town to get supplies," he explained. The Baytons had a handful of male children with pent-up energy, making them a ripe talent pool from which King could initiate members into the Dana gang.

He took a red lighter from his pocket and struck it, lighting his face like he was telling a ghost story.

"We lit them kerosene lines," King said, recalling the

gang's first victory. He swooped his hands like a bellows. His voice rose like he could still see the fire, and his eyes glowed.

King and the Dana street gang had trapped a Vermillion County sheriff's deputy in this very alley. The gang poured kerosene lines at either end and lured him in with taunting. When the deputy drove in, the boys flipped a Zippo and lit the lines, surrounding the patrol car with fire. The deputy jumped out of the car, and the gang stoned him with rocks and eggs and tomatoes and anything not tethered to the ground. The cop ran, defeated.

King launched off his bike and jerked around like the deputy had, trying to dodge the boys' attacks. The haunted alley seemed to erupt with flames and cackling boys.

"No-good pig!" King called like the cop was still there, shouting into the dark. He got back on Leuge's bike. We followed him down the alley, yearning for streetlights.

We returned to paved streets as King pointed out every house the street gang had hit with lit paper sacks of dog shit. They rang doorbells on dilapidated wooden porches and dashed to a safe distance, where they could get a good look at the victim stomping out smelly turds. It felt tame in comparison with setting a cop car on fire, but then King paused to examine a wreck of a house barely standing.

"Watch it, girls. Might get electrocuted," he said, pointing to the burnt-up front yard. "Old Man Riley tried to fry us. No-good SOB hated us." King motioned toward the back, where Riley's outhouse had been, now an overgrown lot. "He was hosing off them dentures." The street gang had tipped Riley's latrine one night with him in it, making his ill-fitting teeth land in his own shit. King mimed an octogenarian watering off his own smile with a hose, then popping his teeth back in. Riley then installed the fence.

"Riley was a GD bully!" he said. "Just like Breezo the Clown."

In silence, he rolled away from Riley's toward the Methodist church on the east side of town. We were left to wonder who Breezo was as we ventured to Dana's only park next to the church, serving as a landmark of what used to be the Dana school, home to the Dana Aggies. The Lewman brothers went to school there until King's ninth-grade year and Leuge's sixth. When the Vermillion County schools consolidated, the boys were bused to Clinton, where city kids wanted nothing to do with Dana scum.

"We don't *want* you here," King said, mimicking how the Clinton kids shouted at the Dana hicks when they got off the bus. But as the Dana gang defended itself among enemies, their tactics became more dangerous. Harassment turned into knife-throwing contests that led to blades stuck in doorjambs, inches from teachers' ears.

And back in town, the Dana street gang took care of its own bullies.

King described the fight of their lives: defeating Breezo the Clown.

King and Leuge orchestrated the Bayton boys in a payback lashing at the Dana school basketball courts after Breezo beat King on the west side of the Lewman Museum yard and kicked Leuge in the privates during a pickup game. Breezo was big for his age, and with his first offensive move at the court, Leuge cracked him across the back with a baseball bat, and Breezo was restrained by the desperate siblings who shared one toothbrush. Anyone who'd been on the receiving end of bloody battles with Breezo was encouraged to get in a free lick, and as the bully tried to escape the pile-on of sweaty adolescent boys, the Dana gang beat him for a block and a half down the alley. He crawled home as they thrashed him with punches and gut kicks. His mom was waiting at the storm door.

"Lesson number five, girls: Never let a bully get away with it," he said.

King showed my cousins and me that there was no landmark on the midnight bike ride without memories of viciousness.

Violence, it turns out, comes in all forms. Every corner of the town retold the ruthlessness of our fathers' Vermillion County upbringing: Tiger's torture and death, the deputy's trap, vengeful octogenarians, and bullies. Even their own living room was beset with violence. As sure as Grandmother's whip hung on the wall, King and Leuge had a childhood unmatched by any late-night miniseries we knew we were too young to watch on cable. But in the dim streetlights of Dana, we could see that the miracle was that they'd survived it. They faced it through stories reenacted from the safety of sweaty bike seats. As much as they avoided talking about feelings or processing conflict, the Lewman brothers now had their own exposure therapy program, spinning strings of adolescent violence into gold. I didn't yet know the value of it.

We panted and stuck to our sweaty seats as we imagined Breezo's beating, the security of our own childhood summers standing in stark contrast to the Lewman boys' past.

"Pharisees!" King shouted to a dark building when we passed Dana Community Bible Church, where our grandparents were charter members.

"Lock the doors! Keep the sinners out!" King always said.

When I wasn't watching *Hour of Power* with King and the Lady, I was at Sunday school with Lindah and Doggy and at worship with G&GL. Our grandparents were firm in making us attend church every Sunday and Wednesday, but as soon as the hymnals slammed shut, we crossed the Wabash River bridge for Montezuma strawberry fluff at Janet's Restaurant. Some Sundays, Grandmother made family meals, and we all gathered at her dining room table, eating her signature dish of candy spaghetti, which was just Chef Boyardee pasta mixed with brown sugar and ketchup.

"It's Chef Boy-AR-dee," she reminded us when we would tout her pasta as the best we'd had.

But more than once, King dressed up as an Orthodox Jewish rabbi and arrived at Sunday morning services driving a semitruck cab.

"Thou shall not trim the corners of thy beard! Leviticus 19:27!" King would yell at Grandmother over lunch.

"You look like a hobo!" she'd retort.

"You look like a pharisee!" he'd reply.

The two of them went round the tree on the religious fanaticism that accompanied King's cult leadership and schizophrenia.

"Keep up, girls," King said to us as we rode our bikes past the church. "We're on a tight schedule."

The lifelong tension between Grandmother and her two eldest offspring first erupted not long after King and Leuge were out of diapers. When they were old enough to dress themselves, Grandmother beat them and cast them out of the house, even in the harsh, windy Indiana winters.

"We wasn't allowed in the house, see," King said, speeding north toward the ball field. "No one was," he called back to us.

"Your grandmother kept her whip on the wall and her furniture covered in plastic. So, we came up here every day."

He shrugged when we neared the ball diamond. "Snow up to our pits," he said, tugging the buckles of his overalls. "Watch that shit ditch," he added as he crossed a culvert and pedaled onto the dirt diamond.

The town of Dana boasted a famous "shit ditch," a gravity-fed sewage-capture system that lined the outfield. During our fathers' childhood, the trench was a child's height deep, making it a convenient locale for foxhole reenactments. The open sewer plan connected us across generations. When we were in diapers, the town's digested dinners still headed toward third base. A few short years after our midnight bike rides, the modern sewage system was installed under the leadership of the official "shit ditch committee."

"Suicide house over there." King held an invisible gun to his temple as he nodded toward the United States Coast Guard station a hundred yards away from the ball field and shit ditch. The girls and I were perplexed as to why western Indiana had a Coast Guard station. But we shrugged it off as just another corn town mystery, like the deadly VX nerve agent plant the adults complained about. The United States military had it built within spitting distance of people's lives.

At the ball field, King explained how no weather—not even an Indiana winter—kept them inside, despite the hazards of spending cold, wet days playing in the sewer. Illness was easy to come by at all seasons of the year, but especially when frigid winds whipped off flat cornfields into trenches full of fecal matter. One winter, Leuge developed an ear infection. The hearing in his left ear never fully returned.

"This way!" King said, guiding us back to the main road that shot through town.

It was hard for us girls to believe this was the same place where King and Leuge had endured violence and neglect. For us, the town of Dana was a sleepy and innocuous haven. For them, it had been dangerous. The juxtaposition of their treacherous winters and our hurtless summers—their childhood and ours—baffled us.

King hopped the cracked sidewalk toward the closed grocery store.

"Don't complain and don't explain," King said, stretching out three fingers on his left hand like a trident. He mocked our grandfather's disability and his mantra. GL was a quiet man who didn't say much—because he couldn't. An anesthesiologist wrecked his vocal cords during a botched intubation for hernia surgery. His voice never returned. Any words he scratched out were hoarse.

"What a load of bull!" King said, dancing around, twitching his eight fingers, and repeating another of GL's mantras in a hoarse voice. King hiked up his overalls the way Grandfather pulled his own trousers far above his waistline. But GL looked nothing like his firstborn son, who was also his namesake. Grandfather wore pressed khakis each day and a crisp button-up shirt rolled up at the sleeves. His gunmetal glasses made him look crabby like photos of Gramps. But he was kind to us girls.

But King's relationship with his father was strained. "Don't complain and don't explain" fell flat on my father, who felt entitled to do both. But this mantra had been the basis on which GL and his nurse bride, our grandmother, started their new life in Dana. The war was over. They saw survival and livelihood: a lucrative corn town a few counties away from where GL had been raised by Gramps, the alleged Wabash murderer. Dana had good soil and a railroad, and it needed a grocery store on Main Street. G&GL ran Regal Grocery Store and four successful farms all with labor from their two eldest sons. The Lewmans rotated corn and soybeans and rolled out miles of fencing all while the boys were school age.

"He worked us to the bone and beat us worse," King explained, putting his bike on its kickstand, throwing his arm back like he was starting a lawn mower, and reenacting the bullwhip beatings.

"One million, two million, three million." He mimicked GL counting bands of cash with three fingers while the boys stocked shelves and sacked groceries for old ladies. King loaded them into cars with an exaggerated limp; Dana's matriarchs stuffed coins into his pocket for tips.

Lewman's Regal Grocery Store relied on the weekly bump from the money that hired farmers spent on Saturdays when they came into town to trade, get haircuts, shop, or "shoot the bull," as King put it. Saturdays in Dana, my father said, had an atmosphere all their own. The local agricultural labor force propped up corn town capitalism until it rotted away when the roads out of Vermillion County improved. But in King's time, the prosperous 1950s were just a hand-mixed Thomas Soda Shop slurp away.

There was cash to be made, and the eldest Lewman boys made it for GL. But King's relationship with his parents was now as bitter as a bad drop. G&GL felt they'd wasted their energy trying to straighten out their eldest son. Dad felt he'd wasted his youth building Grandfather's empire. It was a confusing mix of boyhood sadness and defiance. But it hadn't begun this way. King, after all, had been Grandmother's favorite son. She saw herself in him: wild, reckless, dark hair, quick fuse, and different. When her own father left for a life of gambling and roaming, and then her mother died, Grandmother's feelings of abandonment mirrored those King felt in his own unquiet mind. King and his mother were alike, which made me wonder if that scared her.

I wondered many things that I couldn't ask her. By the time I was born, Grandmother was blond and attentive, a mother-like figure to me, much like Aunt Marietta. Whenever she kept me overnight at their place, I'd watch her stand at the half-open kitchen window in a red cowgirl shirt, her back to me, taking slow draws off a lit cigarette from a green-and-white pack she kept hidden in the bathroom. Lost in thought, she washed dishes as lightning bugs flitted across the indigo yard. She treated herself to a smoke after dinner, despite GL's asthma.

"Grandmother looks *lovely,*" the girls and I would tease one another, mimicking her Savannah accent. She was always put together by 7:00 A.M., with caked Estée Lauder makeup, a wig, huge clip-on earrings, and hot pink lipstick. Grandmother was the kind of woman who took up space. You noticed her. And if you didn't, she'd make sure you redirected your gaze.

There were so many nights when I wanted to ask her about the stories King told on drop trainings and midnight bike rides. Did Gramps really push her husband off a homemade raft into the Wabash River? Why did she and GL beat their children? Instead, I kept quiet while her frosted white nails tapped the ash off her Marlboro into a glass ashtray on the windowsill.

"Oh, for land's sakes," I knew she'd have said, dismissing me with another drag, then humming a few bars of "Moonlight Serenade" in her froggy voice.

When I spent the night with them, I slurped a brown cow so fast my brain turned into a slushy. Then, I was excused to sit at Grandmother's vanity table and play makeup with the

tube of strawberry ChapStick she kept just for us granddaughters. Behind their bedroom door, GL kept a tall gun cabinet
decorated with his Purple Heart. While I blotted my waxy lips,
Grandmother told me war stories. Her official army portrait
showed the chestnut waves I inherited and the chocolate eyes I
didn't. Her rosy lips had seized a few soldiers' hearts. By our
childhood calculations, she'd been engaged thrice.

If it was just the three of us girls, Grandmother would
play 1940s big-band cassette tapes and teach us how to jitterbug. When we were in middle and high school, she drove
us clear to Terre Haute in Vigo County to shop at Honey
Creek Mall, where we begged for nineties overalls that we'd
snap only on one side. Instead, she ushered us through a mandatory tour of her courtship history by way of the men's suits.
With her orange self-tanned legs dancing in the shortest white
shorts I'd ever seen anyone's grandmother wear, she shim-
mied through the suit coats like they were dance partners.
Grandmother plumped the sides of her blond wig and peeled
back the collars until she found him.

"Oh-lay Cay-see-nee," she said, pointing to a tag on a
dapper suit. It was her own version of Italian with a Savannah drawl.

"I dated *him*," she told us.

"Oleg Cassini," we corrected, examining the tag and realizing this was a man and not a euphemism.

"Ay-run Spell-ung," she said, dancing with the next suit.

"Aaron Spelling!" we deciphered.

She had us at "90210" since we worshipped the Beverly
Hills show.

"Kiss me once, then kiss me twice," she belted in the department store. She was the lead act in her own USO show,
with her three granddaughters as captivated audience mem-

bers. Store clerks stopped and stared at a blond grandma with orange legs, dancing with thousand-dollar suits.

When Grandmother reprised her USO act back home in her own living room, we'd see a rare smile from Grandfather. Even as she bragged about these courtships in his presence, he nodded. Since he didn't speak well, it wasn't ever clear if he was corroborating or dismissing. But Cassini had been stationed in Kansas, and Spelling had been in the army during Grandmother's service. These breadcrumbs of Lewman stories—from horse cavalry kill orders to Gramps's river crime to the Underground Railroad entry to stripping teachers to assaults on sheriffs, old men, and bullies—were recounted with such conviction I never knew what to believe.

But the girls and I knew for certain that G&GL had beaten King and Leuge. The proof was in the uneasiness with which King concluded the midnight bike ride by pulling into G&GL's gravel driveway.

Still, my cousins and I knew our grandparents to be mild-mannered though stern military veterans with deep pockets who drove rural routes slowly in a silver minivan we called "the Spit Mobile." Had fate not traded Grandfather's vocal cords for an unending stream of phlegm, we may have seen him as loquacious. Compared with my upbringing in the Ninth Street trailer G&GL seemed tame, even mature, like what I imagined adults should be.

But when the midnight bike ride ended and we walked up the cement stairs with King, the oxygen vanished. Inside, the air didn't have a chemical stench or anything physical that made it hard to breathe. It was an invisible, intuitive tension between G&GL and their eldest son.

We hugged our grandparents and ran to the kitchen to

slurp the brown cows Grandmother had waiting for us at the table. It was a sugary distraction from whatever relational mess the adults were navigating. Grandmother had even made an extra one for King, who reluctantly sat down at the table and sucked up the treat.

But within a minute, King leaped from the dining room table and began dancing around the room like his feet were on fire. Lindah and Doggy giggled. I stared at the bicentennial glass, examining my vanilla ice cream froth.

"For heaven's sake, Rick! Sit down!" Grandmother chided him, a grown man. Her voice dropped an octave, and she repeated herself. He escalated. King giving her hell was as common as the runs in her pantyhose—only now she couldn't reach for the bullwhip.

"You're trying to *kill* me, Dorothy!" King said, pointing at her and grabbing his ribs.

The girls stopped laughing. He was serious. I'd known he was.

"Oh, foot!" Grandmother said. "Sit down, Rick."

"My leever! My leever!" he yelled, cupping his right side and whatever remained of his liver. The girls stared now as King grew more anxious, pacing the room in distress, as if he were in actual pain. But even as a little girl, I knew it was actually *emotional* agony.

Trafficking made King feel invincible. Grandmother made him feel vulnerable. Despite drug drops and cult leadership and street gangs and midnight bike rides, King was still a little boy longing for his mother's attention and instead receiving her displeasure. She was now too old to command a whip. He could have easily killed her right there, snapping her neck like a pencil or shanking her with his knife. I knew he thought about it. But he didn't.

"Do something, Budge. Your devil of a grandmother is trying to kill me!" King said, appealing to me.

Despite my training, I froze. I didn't grab my knife. I didn't cuss my Grandmother out. I didn't threaten to kill her. I left my body, hiding in the melting milk froth of the sweaty glass.

At home in the Ninth Street trailer, I was attentive and empathetic to my parents' pain. In private, I didn't feel the hot shame of other people's judgment. Alone with King and the Lady, I could twist myself into whatever vessel they needed: a listening ear, an eager lookout, or a child who could busy herself with MTV music videos and construction paper and bubble baths. Even in the darkness of our midnight bike rides, I felt less humiliation over King's mental illness, his ticks, his mannerisms, his paranoia, and his outbursts. But here, in the light of G&GL's kitchen, I saw the alarm and discomfort my father's behavior caused in others. It embarrassed me.

"This is it, Budge. I won't be here much longer," King said, reaching out his Vaselined hand and pleading with me to do something. He was about to drop to the floor when Grandfather came into the kitchen.

For the first time ever, GL's voice was thick and strong.

"That's *enough*, Rick," he said, clear as day.

Whatever real or imagined pain King felt evaporated. He shrugged and stomped out of G&GL's place as if to say, *Well, that was fun.*

"Rick's a little crazy, isn't he?" Grandfather said, as if he'd just learned about my father's schizophrenic diagnosis from a doctor's note.

So, in the warm light of our grandparents' kitchen on a summer night, I realized that even while King thrived in a complex lifestyle like trafficking and had the wits, sneakiness, and toughness it took to run gangs and dealers, he melted in the presence of his parents. They made him feel small and shamed, when what he really needed was their love.

As King always said, "You can't fix crazy."

"The definition of insanity is doing the same thing over and over and expecting different results," the Lady liked to add.

King, like most Hoosiers I knew, had a propensity toward a brand of Indiana absurdity that baffled outsiders. Despite degrees and skills and licenses to work anywhere else, my father boomeranged back to Vermillion County like a tetherball strung to a pole. His connection with his hometown and his enmeshment with his child-beating parents were an inch from noxious, like the extra dash of salt that ruins a perfectly good soup.

But I recognized his longing for Vermillion County. It was a yearning for home. I saw it because I longed for it too.

FOUR

Carnival Captivations

NDIANA FALL ARRIVED AND, WITH IT, AN UPTICK IN OUR trafficking business. Viper's gun also made a reappearance in our Ninth Street trailer. I was five and had reluctantly begun kindergarten at Central Elementary School in Clinton.

King had always been averse to large-scale drug trafficking. It wasn't because he had an ethical issue with it, and he wasn't deterred by violence. Instead, it was the responsibility that annoyed him. Inventory, cargo, big trucks, kiddie rides, and cash weighed him down like barbells in his pockets. But the Carnival Captivations kiddie-ride drug-trafficking business was my parents' necessary means to an end.

While sophisticated crime families used time-tested cash businesses to shuffle drugs and wash money, we were just flyover hicks slinging kilos and bricks in play-animal carcasses. The put-on grandiosity of small-town peddlers setting up their doped-up ponies in front of the Kmart was absurd; we were an inch away from being just like the caste of carnies who smoked meth behind Ferris wheels and fed their babies Coca-Cola in the bottle.

"Sweet Corn's meeting us at the farm," King said the day after his fortieth birthday, October 1986. "Got to get your mother up and moving today," he added, pouring coffee into a mug, then scooping up a treat of soft, cheesy scrambled eggs for the Lady. He placed them on the bedside tray, and I followed him as he carried it into the bedroom. We had a big drop planned for the following week, and King wanted us to gather at the farm for our one and only family portrait—a fortieth-birthday present.

"My get-up-and-go done got up and went," the Lady said, head propped on a striped pillow. She wanted to cancel the photoshoot and the trip and stay nestled in the dirty luxury-thread-count sheets we couldn't afford. They had been purchased using her gas credit card. Every year, she made her summer pilgrimage to the Fieldcrest linens store in Eden, North Carolina, her home state.

"Our Lady of Perpetual Recumbency," King told his disciples when they came over for sermons and drugs and asked if she were living.

We coaxed the Lady into taking the coffee and eggs. King laid out her nicest clothes and the new outfit Grandmother had bought me. I got dressed and gushed over her beautiful skin and her photogenic qualities. Even at five, I'd already unconsciously mastered the manipulation technique I'd learned from her: flattery as transaction. Our stroking (plus a dose of amphetamine and Afrin) was enough to pry her from the sheets.

We drove our newest vehicle, a red-and-gray SUV we'd stolen for the winter, to G&GL's acreage outside Dana. Sweet Corn, a Vermillion County harmonica player with a penchant for pills, was waiting for us, his breath visible in the cool air. A bulky camera hung around his neck. The fancy family portrait would be his gift to Dad.

"Good-looking family you got there, King," he said.

Sweet Corn lined us up against the amber trees on Grandfather's land. His camera snapped. I closed my eyes and inhaled Indiana's autumn of decaying leaves, fallow fields, and G&GL's horse hay, then leaned down to feel the damp grass at my feet. Beside my pink boots, there was a rust-colored pillowcase.

King reached for it just as I did.

"Guns are for idiots, little girl," King whispered and patted me on the head. "You stick with your knife." He cradled the pillowcase in the crook of his elbow like a sleeping baby.

Sweet Corn shuffled us around, posing King in his bright yellow rain slicker and the new Lakers cap he got for his birthday. I tugged at my pink scarf, as cozy as the ones in the Lady's L.L.Bean catalogs. My mother looked down at me, unusually happy with clean gray hair slicked back in a bun and cider-colored lips parted in a beauty-pageant smile. She'd come alive on G&GL's farm because she grew up on hundreds of her own father's acres in central North Carolina. To her, land was status. It outclassed the dump of an aluminum single wide on a lot of rented weeds. When you had grass and trees and sky and dirt to call your own, you were somebody. You had a throne.

Sweet Corn arranged our little family for his final shot. In it, King has lowered the rust-colored pillowcase to my right shoulder. It holds Viper's loaded gun, rigid beneath Fieldcrest cotton. My eyes are closed, and my mouth is parted in a genuine smile as if to say, *This is the final frame of my life.*

In a way, it was. Everything was about to change.

The Lady's contentment disappeared as soon as we returned to the Ninth Street trailer. She traded makeup and a smile for a coffee-stained T-shirt and thick glasses. Her exhaustion called her back to bed like she'd carried rocks all day. This was, after all, how the Lady spent most of her Indiana days: catatonic from weed and benzos, riding out her own "college" sentence.

Inasmuch as the Lady thought herself better than King, Vermillion County, and trailer life, she was grandiose enough to believe that she could manifest her uppity nature from the nest of her bed. The world was run from a pillow-top mattress, she thought. And keeping a marriage intact and raising a daughter while watchdogging a high-stakes drug-trafficking scheme was no big deal. But Vermillion County chipped away at her slowly. What I'm uncertain of is whether she was just biding her time, relying on King's childcare until I was old enough to take care of her.

The only activity that interested the Lady was homemade textiles. While she kept watch over the floor-to-ceiling Carnival Captivations inventory hidden behind mirrored closet doors, she crafted manically. Without leaving her soft bed, the Lady knit afghans with a fury and cross-stitched inspiration for our dark-paneled walls. My mother relished the warmth of blankets as she knit them and said prayers as she cross-stitched. But few recipients had need for a Judy Lewman original. Still, the Lady had all her cross-stitching custom-framed with money we couldn't spare. It was a nod to what she felt was her due—wealth marked by original artwork.

The trailer walls were lined with her sayings: "My bifocals fit me well, the dentures are just fine—but, lord, how I miss my mind!" and "Now I lay me down to sleep, I pray the Lord my soul to keep."

"Who's this for?" I asked that afternoon, visiting her in bed, my pink photoshoot scarf still tied around my neck. I pointed to the rectangle block spread across her lap, teal and brown cross-stitch showing "The Lew."

"Your aunt and uncle!" she said, frustrated that I couldn't decipher how "Lew" would be "Lewmans." It didn't matter that I was only five.

"Here," she said, handing me a copy of *Reader's Digest* from a messy heap of *National Geographic* magazines. "Read these."

I sat on the edge of the bed and flipped through magazine pictures. Once I finished, I stacked the periodicals neatly, then fidgeted with her plastic sewing box. Propped up and watching *The 700 Club,* she switched to working on an afghan that was also wrapped around her legs.

"Make yourself useful, young lady," she said, handing me a white plastic tub of buttons, a needle, and a thick piece of cross-stitch string.

"How?" I asked.

"You're smart. You'll figure it out," she said.

While King's "veeshuns" were that I'd follow his Vermillion County legacy, the Lady wanted me to be an educated and classy southern lady. Maybe even a trophy wife. Certainly, an Emily Post enthusiast. But I had no patience for stringing shiny plastic on a thread.

"This is your Duke blanket, Rainbow Girl," she said.

I looked up from the first shiny button I'd managed to string and watched her knit and purl, fuzzy dark blue and white yarn at her fingertips.

"You're going to school there just like your brother!"

I have one sibling from the Lady's first marriage to Dude, a Steady Eddy reliable accountant. Dude and the Lady were married twenty years and had one son, whom we called Achilles, or Lee for short. Mom was twenty-three when Lee was born. Dude went to work and played softball and golf, and she kept house. By the time I was born, Lee was nearly eighteen and leaving home to be a pre-med undergraduate at Duke University.

"Why does my Duke blanket have holes in it?" I asked.

It was just like the rainbow blanket Mom had knit for me to commemorate my California birth narrative.

"This is a proper *afghan* for a proper young lady." She kept knitting, convinced that I would go to Duke too.

But Lee had grown up in an actual house. I lived in a trailer. Trailer kids never got too far.

"This one is next." After finishing a row, she tapped her knitting needle to a cross-stitch pattern of Duke University's crest inscribed with the words *Eruditio et Religio,* referring to the moral, scholarly cultivation of a person.

"*Eruditio et Religio,*" she bellowed. "I'm a poet and don't know it!

"Your father is *so* good with you," she said as I strung more buttons during an episode of *Larry King Live.* "He's been working your legs since birth! And building those arms too."

When I was an infant, King would pedal my feet like I was on a stationary bike. The first time I rolled over, he duct-taped rags to my knees so I could keep going without getting rug burn and clean the floors at the same time. The Lady's goal for me was calorie burning; King's was raising a street fighter.

When even gang members emblazoned with satanic tattoos and known by street names like Meatsweat balked at my baby-bottle duct-taped hands and my duct-taped kneepads, King assured them, "Training her up for battle!"

"For God's sakes, Rick, you *train* elephants," the Lady would shout from the back bedroom. "You're *educating* her."

The afternoon I learned how to string a button, the phone rang. I picked up. "Hello. Lewmans'," I said, mimicking Aunt Marietta. It was Viper.

King was busy entertaining and preaching to his disciples in the living room. It didn't matter. Viper wanted to discuss something with the Lady.

"You're a gentleman and a scholar," she said into the phone. "I wouldn't mind it one bit. Just got to convince Peter Pan."

She hung up, confident.

"Wouldn't you just *love* to live on a farm?" the Lady said to me after the call. "You loved being out at your grandfather's place this morning, didn't you?"

I nodded.

"Well, Viper wants to buy us a big farmhouse! Isn't that nice? Now, you've got to convince your father to get us out of *here*. Just look at this dump." She scrunched her nose and gestured toward the indestructible plastic walls like they were crumbling. "Hot and cold running rats!"

But my parents had bought this brand-new trailer on credit three years earlier. The Lady knew she'd need me to help coax King into taking the upgrade she and Viper were hoping to entice him with.

Viper wanted to move us from the Ninth Street trailer out into the country, where we'd have some acreage. There, we could store and move more inventory with privacy. More bricks and mortar meant more bricks and bales. We could leave behind this dump with its piddly trunk drops and weeded lot. The Lady could watchdog barns instead of closets. Our water heater could be covered with cash.

"And we could get away from the *undesirables,*" the Lady said. She was talking about King's entourage and our neighbor, whom she and King called "Boozy Piddler," or BP for short. BP was a scruff of a man with perpetual bedhead and a proclivity for "the sauce."

"Tell your father you want a farmhouse. You've got him wrapped around your little finger." She barely looked up from her knitting. "God watches over fools *and* children," she added.

But I knew King wouldn't want to leave Clinton—let alone Vermillion County. His contentious relationship with G&GL meant we'd never live within Dana town limits again, even though he loved Dana. And King liked the Ninth Street party trailer full of his devotees and drugs. Country living would mean his disciples would have to go out of their way to sit at the feet of their guru. Besides, he didn't mind rotating inventory out of the mirrored closet for a trunk drop. He'd gotten into the habit of duct-taping bands of cash to his chest, and wearing more than ten thousand dollars made him paranoid.

But even King's gang members had grown concerned about him taking me on drug drops.

"You're taking her *again*?" I once heard Meatsweat ask. He wasn't implying that my parakeet lookout skills were lacking. Rather, this was a tough-as-nails midwestern man who disapproved of Viper and King leveraging my innocuous runt look and secret ability to explode. He knew that as the kilos and cash grew, so did the danger.

Still, I hadn't agreed to say anything to King about the farmhouse, so the Lady resorted to more aggressive tactics. "We don't even have two pennies to rub together," she said, exasperated.

She scooted her knitted purls along the thick needle like an abacus and gave me a hard stare. "Look around. We're in the poorhouse, for goodness' sakes. Is that what you want?"

In those days, the only legal money my parents earned was from covers.

"To keep the feds off my sack," King would say, cashing the one-hundred-dollar check he got from mowing grass at the golf club. Every other Friday, he picked up his check and drank it at Dreamland bar.

The Lady asked him to quit the golf course. She was sapped from the bi-monthly effort it took to pick up King's measly paychecks before he could drink them. If she didn't get to them first, she lost out on the entrepreneurial capital she said she needed to start her own business. She'd just quit her own short-lived nursing job at Vermillion County's only hospital to "raise a family." In truth, the Lady resigned before she could be fired for failing to respond to a patient's medical emergency.

"It's not the job of a head nurse to do those types of things. That's a *staff* duty," the Lady told King after she walked out on the patient's code. "That woman had the nerve to tell me, 'It's an all-hands-on-deck type of thing.' I beg to differ." The Lady, still in her uniform, sat down at her Smith Corona typewriter and banged out a scathing letter: *I believe you will continue to get caught in your own web of manipulation in your pursuit of power. This railroading attempt toward me was a very sinister and unnecessary example of your manipulations. I decline to participate in your games.*

The Lady burned Vermillion County bridges as fast as Gramps had dumped her husband into the Wabash.

She hopped one county over for a nursing-home job, where she was quickly fired.

"If you didn't run your goddamn mouth so much," King said, arguing with her when she was fired again.

"If a frog had wings, it wouldn't bump its butt!" she said. "If you weren't a no-good who spent your check as fast as you earned it."

"How do you expect me to grease the wheels?" King said to her. "It's all about who you knows."

But what the Lady wanted was the farmhouse, barns bursting with inventory and bathtubs full of cash.

"You've got to convince your father to get us out of here," she repeated. "This place is a dump."

As I strung buttons on her bed, I knew we were low on funds. We always were. The empty refrigerator and the gifts of clothes, shoes, and toys from Grandmother and Aunt Marietta told me that. But I knew we lived in a brand-new-trailer-turned-dump because my parents didn't clean or do laundry. They hung towels over windows with safety pins hooked to nails.

I reached for the sky-blue stationery next to the Lady's copy of Tony Robbins's *Unlimited Power*.

"Don't touch that, young lady! It's for my mail-order business," she explained, snatching it out of my hand and running her fingers over the textured *JTL Enterprises* in block letters printed on luxury paper.

"I need time and space to run my business. There's no room here." Every inch of their room was covered in papers, textiles, clothes, or cough-drop wrappers.

My parents believed that money was for spending and that people were dumb enough to spend theirs on something we had to offer. From King's drugs and kiddie rides to the Lady's entrepreneurialism, their schemes were built on the premise that people had cash to burn. Maybe that was true. But what

was more perplexing was what happened to the cash that customers gave us.

"Do this for me, would you? Remember that nice sleeping bag Viper got you?" she said. "The world owes you nothing, Dana. You owe the world everything."

I finished stringing my buttons in silence.

The Lady's farmhouse campaign persisted for days. Her
mission to manipulate King drove her out of bed like a feisty
hamster. The day after she appealed to me, her dull eyes
sharpened. She got dressed every day and fluttered about the
house. "I'm as anxious as a polecat," she told me.

Her spurt of energy coincided with the first and only kiddie-
ride drug drop we made as a family. A week after Sweet Corn's
photoshoot, Viper rented us a fancy truck hitched to a flatbed
trailer. We were slated to cross state lines; the Lady thought it
would be the final trafficking task before our move to a country
farmhouse with more barn space than we could imagine. The
deal was simple: Viper would help us stay put on that land—no
more kiddie-ride drops—in exchange for storing more inventory
onsite. The Lady was exuberant; King was uninterested.

Looking back, I can see that King was right to be suspicious. While the Lady took his apathy for laziness, he was the
smarter criminal. More drugs in one place was a recipe for
"college" or worse.

During that drop, we spent two nights on the road. I remember it only because I can still see the chocolate pie we ate
on take-out Styrofoam plates. Viper gave us cash for food,
and on my third day with a full belly, I heard "Glory of Love"
from *The Karate Kid Part II* for the first time on the radio. As
we pulled into the warehouse, I watched the late-October
orange-sherbet sunset and played the MTV music video in my
mind, relishing a quiet, full tummy.

"Let's go, Budge!" King yelled, motioning me to get out of the cab. Inside the warehouse, shiny ponies stood in rows. There were more than my preschool-dropout numbers lessons would allow me to count. Our voices echoed, and my hands glided across brand-new glittery hydraulic ponies as shiny as the cheap nail polish I used as paint on my construction paper. I had just stepped onto the diamond-tread base to straddle a purple mare when King saw me.

"I will pop you, knucklehead," he shouted from the trailer bed, where he and a worker unloaded our trailer.

Besides the fact that it wasn't covered in rust, the horse seemed no different from our single wide's metal hitch, which I often pretend-galloped on like a jockey in the Preakness.

He ran over to pull me off just as I was about to settle on the fiberglass saddle.

"That ain't no toy!" he yelled.

But it was. Kiddie rides were playthings for every kindergartner but me. These fairy-dusted animals were Saturday morning cartoons come to life. They beckoned kids and quarters. Children across the country would ride these. Except me.

"You've got a job to do, young lady," King snapped. "Get over here." He pointed to my mark, then dog-collared my neck with his hand and positioned me at the door. "Right here. Eyes open."

In the last slivers of that autumn day, I didn't feel tough or strong or prepared to explode like I had the night in the woods when I was relegated to the stairs with the stuffed cat. Here, the sun was bright enough to make me squint. I kicked at the fresh gravel and looked up at the steel doors. Inside, the rides beckoned to me: A bright blue pony with a silver saddle and exaggerated horse teeth seemed to say, *Come ride me!*

From the entrance, I saw the Lady walk around the warehouse like she was examining her empire. Her shoulders pushed back and her head held high, she was dressed in expensive L.L.Bean khakis and a cheerful polo. The Lady didn't lift a finger; she just strutted, nodding, as if she and Viper had been the ones to fill a warehouse with rides that would take drugs and money to the ends of the earth. Then she caught a glimpse of King and sneered. Shuffling drugs in fiberglass carcasses before the age of ubiquitous video surveillance was a piece of chocolate cake compared with how my parents dealt—or didn't deal—with each other's mental illnesses.

I went back to work.

The warehouse doors opened like those on Grandfather's pole barn, and I stayed at my post, squinting in the golden hour. King and the Lady handled business until dark. Then they shuffled me back into the truck Viper had rented for us. I never did get to ride one of those ponies.

November arrived, and the Indiana skies turned as dull as Sheetrock. The Lady continued to spend more time out of bed and at the kitchen counter with King. She took my chopping place, and in the evenings, I was sent to my room to watch MTV. After dark, I heard them cackling about their psych patients, the keys, the pilgrimage to Los Angeles, and their mutual enemies. They smoked whatever drugs were left over from the day and listened to bootleg tapes of Dr. Don, a synthesized-jazz DJ.

"We have a good time, don't we?" I heard King say to the Lady.

"Just like we've got good sense!" she said, and they laughed.

It was their call-and-response when they felt at peace.

In those moments, I made the mistake of feeling like a child again.

I was left out of their banter but lulled by the false coziness of the impending winter and the security it seemed to bring. Maybe they had worked out the farmhouse offer on their own. Maybe the warm light and the saxophones and the euphoria of two adults relishing their drugs as the days grew shorter meant we were going to have full bellies for a while. Though I was lonely and missed being my father's sidekick, it was a break from the intensity of King's mania and the Lady's depression.

I'm unsure now if those nights were simply the Lady's way of manipulating King into the farmhouse plan. Getting out of bed and dressed, showing King affection, spending time with him—was it all a ruse to get him to accept Viper's offer? Maybe she really thought it would work.

But King's superpower—the side effect of his paranoid schizophrenia—was that he distrusted everyone and everything. My father wouldn't be outmanipulated, which made the Lady desperate.

Viper lined up a pickup and drop, this one for mid-November. It was big, he said. Complicated. Dangerous. All the way to upstate New York, near the Canadian border.

"I want to go!" I whined to King.

"Not this time, Budge. Just me and your mom," he said.

The Lady was now my competition for King's affection and attention. I'd failed to convince him to take Viper's deal, so the Lady inched me out. They packed my bag for G&GL's.

My parents gave me uneasy hugs in my grandparents' doorway. King insisted I be good for G&GL; the Lady seemed distracted. They pulled out of the gravel drive in another Dodge truck, this one the same blue as the Lady's Duke afghan. I sulked as Grandmother sat me at her kitchen table, relieved to have me close for a few days of brown cows and playdates with Doggy and Lindah. My cousins arrived; we rushed to the large wicker trunk Grandmother stocked full of her hand-me-downs for dress-up. For hours, we reenacted Saturday night TV shows like *Hee Haw* and *The Golden Girls*, trying different combinations of Grandmother's digs until we effectively became Dorothy, Rose, and Sophia. We left Blanche to Grandmother. That night, Grandfather showed us the used pinball machine he'd bought to entertain us, and we were in heaven.

I felt at home.

Thursday night, I went to bed full and happy, stuffed with candy spaghetti and brown cows, cousin play, and back-to-back *The Cosby Show, Family Ties, Cheers,* and *Night Court.* But in the middle of the night, I peeled off the polka-dot sheets and looked out the window to the driveway. G&GL's yard was midnight dark. In that moment, I missed my parents and wondered if they'd be able to complete the drop without me.

It may have been the very same moment the Lady decided to punch the gas. Somewhere near the Canadian border, my parents hit a record-breaking November snowfall. The Lady was driving, a fact I found troubling when I later learned about it. Her warm southern upbringing made her an inexperienced navigator in low temps and limited visibility. But while King smoked and wrestled maps, she was behind the wheel, cursing the inches of snow.

Between the pressure of picking up kiddie rides full of drugs at the border and being put upon to drive, she boiled over. She floored it, and they barreled off a snowy embankment in Viper's truck. Unrecognizable twists of burnt metal and flurries of glass were all that remained when a state trooper found them sitting on the shoulder.

"Lucky to be alive," the officer said.

My parents were silent.

Lucky to have wrecked an empty truck.

States away, I slid back between cold sheets and fell into an uneasy sleep. The smell of Grandmother's maple brown-sugar oatmeal woke me up the next morning. It wasn't a mirage like my mother's blueberry muffins. It was real and nurturing and piping hot, set next to a tall glass of chocolate milk. And Grandmother was there to greet me with a big hug.

I stayed with them for two nights. Just as I began to allow myself to fall into the rhythm of safety and home and being cared for by loving adults, G&GL got a call to drop me off at the Ninth Street trailer.

I could tell Grandmother was reluctant to take me back to my parents.

The Lady was back in bed, depressed and cross-stitching. King was at the counter, reading his King James Bible through dime-store glasses. His ball cap was off, and for the first time, he seemed old.

"Missed you, Budge," he said when I walked in. "Go check on your mom."

I put down my overnight bag and felt my way down the dark-paneled hallway.

"Come sit," the Lady said, tapping the bed. "Your father is *psychotic!*" she added. "He was going to let us die in Buffalo, New York, of all places."

She told me that, near the border, she gave up, seemingly on everything. As a whiteout blasted them and inches of snow piled up, she floored it and drove right off the road. On purpose. "I had to do something," she said, shrugging like she was surrounded by idiots.

They didn't complete the pickup and drop. Instead, she destroyed Viper's brand-new truck. They never made it to the warehouse. Looking back now, I realize one redemptive thread in her stupidity: Had the state trooper found them after they were loaded up, they'd have spent at least a dime apiece in "college." Maybe a whole lot more.

I suspect she thought they wouldn't survive any of it—the pickup, the drop, the threat of a prison term. But because they had made it back from Buffalo, her suicide attempt turned into a hero's victory in her mind. She was the one who had preempted their fate—maybe a head-on collision or a "college" sentence—by purposefully running the entire rig off the road.

The Lady smashed it without caring that I might have been orphaned.

"I saved us," she said. "You'll thank me one day."

It wasn't salvation. It was a schism. The Lady wanted to be out of drops, tucked away, cozy, set up in Viper's farmhouse. King wanted the Lady to stay out of it.

As they fought over the future of our involvement in Carnival Captivations, I became a chess piece to both. The Lady tried to get me to help her in her farmhouse coup, but I'd been my father's daughter first, raised to chop, drop, and traffic.

My mother's supposedly salvific Buffalo wreck was a record she played on repeat. It was just one in a long line of sacrifices she'd made. The Lady recounted them to us, beginning with quitting her Rollman psychiatric nursing job to sit at the feet of Dr. Schuller in L.A. A cross-country move, having a baby at age forty-one, financial strain, living in Vermillion County, saving us from being murdered by Viper's gun—all these sacrifices indebted King and me to her. She kept a tally of transactions, and we'd drained our account.

I realize now that this was her mental illness. Her diagnoses made it impossible for her to be aware of how she kept this kind of tally. The Lady's dependent personality disorder caused continual havoc. King's schizoaffective disorder led his brain to make poor choices during my first five years of life. The only difference between the two was that his symptoms were unmistakable.

FIVE

The Notebook Method of Divorce

W E'RE HEADED TO CINCY!" THE LADY CROWED ONE late June morning in our Ninth Street trailer. I had just turned six years old.

By then, Viper had taken the farmhouse deal off the table. My parents had botched a border drop. King was losing interest in Carnival Captivations. And drug bosses were losing patience with us.

The Lady had stayed in bed all winter and spring, having given up on the farmhouse, while King and I continued making our piddly trunk drops without her. Then, one early summer morning, the Lady woke up, got dressed, left the house, and came back with a brand-new '98 Oldsmobile. She put our silverware in the trunk. The Lady had made "vacation plans" on the pretext of showing me her old stomping grounds in Ohio and North Carolina.

I was playing with the driver's side seat buttons when our neighbor BP waddled home and swayed up his front stoop.

King walked down the rusted stairs and over to the car, wearing a white undershirt, sweatpants, and no hat. "Budge, you be good for your mom," he said.

"You're such a good travel buddy," the Lady said as I studied the pee patterns on BP's pants. "Not like when you were three months old and we drove cross-country from L.A. *You* decided to get colicky in Colorado. You cried that entire trip! *Every. Single. Mile.* Worry a body to death!" She rolled her eyes.

King reached out to hug me. His arms were scaly, missing his daily coating of Vaseline. Wherever we were headed, he wasn't going.

In the early-morning sun, there in Vermillion County, King seemed sad. I realize now that he never mentioned a reunion—there was no promise of midnight bike rides, Dairy Queen chocolate malts, or working together. There wasn't even a "See you soon." He dog-collared my neck and steered me over to the car, then buckled me into a seatbelt for the first time in my life.

I don't remember that my parents hugged.

The Lady got in and started up the car. We pulled away from the trailer, and King raised a hand to wave, looking defeated.

"Oh, don't be sad," the Lady said.

As we sped past green rows of corn on Ninth Street, I turned on the radio to put my smooth-as-butter tuning into practice.

"I've got to concentrate," my mom said and snapped the radio off.

I slumped down in the new gray velour seats.

She handed me a map depicting all the veins and arteries of the Midwest.

"What's this?" I asked.

"A map! You're smart. You'll figure it out."

We drove east toward Ohio in the brand-new Olds my mother had put on credit.

By age six I'd developed car sickness, a fact King knew. He always let me stare out the window and listen to music, no matter where we were headed. Now I laid the map on my chest, trying to tame the headache building and the wave of vomit coming up my throat.

"I'll just have to figure it out myself," she grumbled.

"Penny for your thoughts?" the Lady cooed as we entered Indianapolis.

What was on my mind was King. Why wasn't he with us? And why did I have to hold a map that would make me barf on the dashboard, which was missing King's signature crucifix?

She snapped on the radio as a peace offering.

"I've seen dark skies, never like this," Eric Clapton sang.

It was the theme song from Martin Scorsese's *The Color of Money*. The same fall Sweet Corn took our family photo at G&GL's farm, my parents took me to see the movie—the first film I ever saw in a theater. It was rated R. "Luck itself is an art!" King repeated one of the opening lines as we squinted in the sunlight after the matinée.

"Luck is where opportunity meets preparation," the Lady said, making edits to Scorsese's script.

"My Budge is gonna be a pool shark! I'll teach you how to hustle money from every dumb motherfucker in this county," King said. "Would you like that?"

I nodded and held his hand.

If luck is an art where opportunity meets preparation, I never knew who held the advantage in our family. Who out-calculated whom?

The Olds rolled across the Ohio border. Rows of corn-fields blurred together. I reached up to my hair for the uncon-scious yet soothing twist-pop-pull motion that always eased my worries. The Lady slapped my fingers away, and the car swerved. I was jolted from the ride, the music, my thoughts.

"Dana, that's not for ladies," she fussed.

"They want to know why we have so much hair around here," the Lady had said one snowy day after she hired a car-pet cleaner to shampoo the trailer shag with money we didn't have. "I told them, 'Because I refuse to vacuum.'" She smiled, gleeful that someone else had to deal with the dirty remnants of her daughter's hair pulling. The brand-new Electrolux sweeper she'd put on her credit card was tucked away in the closet.

Grandmother had tried to cure me of my hair pulling, which had started years before when I was barely potty-trained. That winter when the Lady was in bed, Grand-mother had dolled me up in a vermilion-red dress with tiny white flowers, white tights, and brown shoes. Fluffing my coif for a Sears photographer, she created an illusion of side-swept hair. But no camera magic could hide what had be-come my half mullet. I was beginning a lifelong struggle with a body-focused repetitive behavior (BFRB) called trichotil-lomania, a maladaptive coping mechanism for anxiety and stress.

There in the car, I dropped my hand to the map on my lap and closed my eyes.

As we pulled into Cincinnati, "Everybody Wants to Rule the World" played on the radio. "Welcome to your life. There's no turning back," the lyrics rang.

The Lady had lived in Cincy for more than twenty years.

For a woman who never left our trailer, she was remarkably unfazed by traffic or skyscrapers.

I'd never seen either.

When we walked into the Westin Cincinnati, I fidgeted with a brandy snifter of maroon-and-cream matchbooks on the concierge's desk. The Lady shot me a look. "Pretty is as pretty does," she said, sliding her gasoline credit card over to the woman in a pressed navy blue suit.

"When are we going home?" I asked.

She shushed me. "I'm trying to do business."

The hotel lobby buzzed with people. Under dim lights, they chatted and laughed like they were trying to impress one another at a cocktail party, the clink of glasses and soft piano music underscoring their sophistication.

We took an elevator to our room overlooking the hotel fountain. It reminded me of the cracked white concrete of the four-seasons fountain at the Wabash River near the Dairy Queen. Already, I missed King and our chocolate malts.

"Can we get Dairy Queen?" I asked.

"*Dairy Queen*? Wouldn't you just love a fresh cup of coffee?" She handed me a white summer dress Grandmother had bought me. After I put it on, we went down to the hotel's restaurant. I wore dresses only for G&GL's Christmas Eve parties and the Sears portrait. As I fidgeted in my seat, she sipped her steaming coffee from a porcelain cup. She ordered German chocolate pie served on fine china. It reminded me of the pie on the Styrofoam plate we'd had on the autumn *Karate Kid* drop.

"Have some, young lady," she said, pushing the pie plate toward me.

"I *hate* that!" I said, shaking my head at the coconut bits.

She corrected my uncouth refusal: "I do *not* care for any, thank you.

"I've got a surprise for you!" the Lady said as I tugged at my dress.

We paid our bill with the credit card and walked back through the busy lobby out onto the street. She opened the glass door of the next high-rise, and the smell of chemicals rushed into my nose. The hair salon was brimming with city women getting foil highlights and full dye jobs.

"You're getting a perm, young lady!" she announced.

I didn't know what a perm was, but I sat dutifully in the chair she pointed to. I was certain it cost money, because this was the kind of place frequented by rich people on TV. We'd already spent money on gas and a hotel room and coffee and pie. I also didn't want anyone touching my twist-pop-pulled hair.

"This will cure you of that *awful* habit of yours," she said.

The permanent solution burned my scalp. For two hours, I sat there on fire, with no escape possible for me and my thin chestnut hair, which was turning blond from the chemicals.

Pain is the brain killer, I remembered, and ten-hutted my way through what I took to be my own hot-box experience, a reminder of King's military torture in a metal coffin with lighters held to his feet.

"Never face a kill room," King had said.

And here I was, glued to a pleather chair, as my mother killed off a remnant of my father's daughter, Budgie.

We left the salon. My new curly hair was dry and fluffy, and I reached up to twist-pop-pull it. But then I stopped. The perm had cost my mother money. While I didn't consider myself valuable in my own right, if someone invested their time and money in me, I didn't want to ruin the outcome. My arms fell to my sides.

The Lady retrieved her Polaroid camera from her big leather bag and asked a stranger to take our photo at the Westin fountain.

I stood on the edge of the fountain as the Lady hugged me. I noticed how thin she was, with her hair perfectly curled and makeup applied. In the photo her brown eyes are on fire. The city had ignited her.

By the next morning, her energy had evaporated. She was propped up in bed like in the Ninth Street trailer, disappointed that the sun had risen. The slight manic high she'd felt from spending money on dinner and our expensive night's stay had dissolved. All that remained of the evening before was the chemical stench of my newly permed hair.

We flung Mom's brown leather American Tourister luggage into the Olds trunk next to the forks and knives and spoons. Back on the road, the Lady was no longer invigorated by Cincy. The fancy hotel was in our rearview, along with its buzzing people and lit fountain. Even the meals eaten in an ornate restaurant were quickly forgotten. Instead, we were just us—Indiana hillbillies pretending to be rich as Roosevelts.

Our destination was Ocean Isle, North Carolina, where the Lady's eldest two brothers, Uncle Charlie and Uncle Elton, owned a condo near the beach that they rented out during the summer months. If there was a freebie to be had, money to be borrowed, or a chance to overstay, my mother sniffed it out. It was a theme of her life that her siblings later shared with me: the Lady, holding court, expecting her needs to be anticipated and met.

"Help the poor!" was her motto, and it was said with

gusto and outstretched hands—a clarion call for food, shelter, money, *anything*.

For three days, we stayed alone at her brothers' place. Lulled by the shore and mother-daughter Polaroids, I played in the sand and posed while she coached me on my beauty-queen posture. She sat in a tide pool, looking melancholy. The beach reminded her of better days.

The morning we were supposed to leave, a severe storm warning was issued for the area. The Lady didn't want to drive in bad weather, but my uncles were firm: Their renters were coming, and the place had to be empty.

"The weather will be fine," Uncle Elton said as she fussed at him over the phone. "You'll be fine," he repeated.

We checked into the Holiday Inn on the beach because the thought of heading wherever we were supposed to go had jarred my mother.

While I bounced on the bed, I tried to refresh her memory that we were a family of three and that our home was in Indiana. "Remember the time we had a sleepover at the Renatto?" I said, trying to cheer her up with memories of me and King.

"I hope you realize now that that place is *trash*," she said. "Hot and cold running rats! And stop jumping on the bed! You'll ruin the sheets. I'm trying to concentrate."

I took out some hand-me-down Barbies my cousins had given me and kept myself occupied reenacting story lines from *Hunter*, which King and I watched on Saturday nights.

Suddenly I heard the Lady making a long-distance call from the bedside phone. "That can't be right." Her voice was shrill. "He can't do that!"

"Is it Dad?" I asked.

"Be quiet!" she said. "I'm doing business."

She finally hung up, defeated. "That no-good manic-depressive canceled my cards! Your father is psychotic!"

"Make yourself useful," she said then, waving me off.

While the Lady examined her math scribbled on the hotel notepad, adding up the wreck of her money, I shrugged and put on my bathing suit, still damp from when I'd packed it at my uncles' place.

King had never withheld the gospel of business or violence, but he was distinctly more reserved about what he was thinking when it came to his marriage or his next move. I didn't know what a manic-depressive was, but I remembered the last time she'd called King psychotic was when he'd botched the Buffalo border drop.

I also knew that my mother relied on that little plastic card for "doing business," and I liked the soothing *swoosh* cashiers made when they pressed it into the carbon copy. While King worshipped at the altar of cash—which could be laundered and left no paper trail—the Lady said that paper bills were something poor people clung to.

The Holiday Inn towels didn't look like anyone had used them to mop up after a knife fight like the ones at the Naughty Renaughty. I took one and left the Lady in the hotel room waiting by the phone. The elevator glided down to a floor with signs that showed a stick figure swimming in a pool. A bubbling Jacuzzi caught my eye.

My hot-tub backstroke was steady when the Lady found me thirty minutes later. She was exasperated that she'd had to look. But she knew where I would be.

Besides pulling my hair, movement and water were my other coping mechanisms. I'd been swimming in the Ninth

Street trailer bathtub every night for my entire life. When my father realized I had the "water bug," he encouraged me.

The winter after my first lessons, I took part in a YMCA swim meet. For the race, Grandmother bought me a black-and-gold Speedo. I won first place for a twenty-five-meter freestyle. I'd crushed the bigger, older kids in one lap. When I climbed out of the pool and realized I'd won, I walked the proudest I ever had past clapping parents who whispered, "That little girl just *won*."

The coach told my parents that that race was the start of a very successful swim career.

Instead, I was now half a continent away from that life, lapping in Jacuzzi bubbles.

"Ma'am," a maintenance man said, approaching my mother as she walked toward the hot tub. "That your kid? She's swimming in diarrhea. Some numbskull got sick last night in that tub."

I ignored them both, micro-lapping in brown froth.

"Dana! Out! Now!"

I slouched out of the water to overhear my mother yelling at the man for not putting up an out-of-order sign; I couldn't have read it yet anyway.

The man's words reminded me of King and his midnight bike ride warnings about the shit ditch in north Dana.

She dragged me back to our room to scrub the filth off me.

I missed King.

But by the end of the night, she had more to worry about than my swimming in hepatitis A.

Fresh from the Holiday Inn shower, I said, "Want a cheeseburger?" I handed Mom an empty glass ashtray in the hope that she'd remember our good times at the Naughty Renaughty with King.

"You tell that no-good son of yours to call me, Dorothy," the Lady yelled into the beige receiver. "I'm not playing games."

It took the Lady several Holiday Inn nights and long-distance phone calls to sort out that King had canceled all their gas credit cards. She'd put everything on credit: the Olds, our hotel, our meals. We were broke and stranded states away from the Ninth Street trailer.

My brother, Achilles, from the Lady's first marriage lived in central North Carolina. At that time, Lee was a twenty-four-year-old medical student at Duke. He shared an apartment with classmates, but that didn't deter the Lady. She decided we could move in with him.

The Lady's lifelong reputation for fiscal stupidity, coupled with warnings from his father, Dude, had made Lee efficient with money. When Dude died of lung cancer when Lee was just nineteen, my brother invested his money in his dream of becoming a doctor. He paid for medical school on his own, all while managing to lend the Lady and King tens of thousands of dollars in the 1980s. Lee had even footed the gas money for King and the Lady to get back to Indiana from California the summer I had colic. Lee's affection and care for me were evident from the day I was born: Polaroids of us together show a happy sibling bond cemented by the shared experience of a troubled mother who was incapable of knowing how sick she was.

It didn't matter that the Lady was draining Lee financially. Mom felt entitled to Dude's money.

"I signed and handed over *all* my inheritance checks to Dude when my father died," the Lady told me, as if Lee, by proxy, was obligated to return that money to her now.

One out of every three calls to her firstborn was to ask for more.

"Rick doesn't want to see us right now," the Lady told

Lee, unpacking the Olds into his apartment while I occupied myself with North Carolina pine needles, which I'd never seen before. She implied that it was temporary and that we'd be back in the car and Indiana-bound in no time.

But a marriage between two mentally ill drug addicts that begins in a psych hospital is bound to end in madness.

"That wedding was a blur," Lee told me decades later. He was fifteen when King and the Lady got married at G&GL's, and my parents snorted cocaine in celebration. The Lady had abandoned Lee and his father, Dude, just a year earlier.

That first night at Lee's apartment, the Lady left in the Oldsmobile. I kept myself entertained with pens and paper my brother gave me, nurturing my love of art.

She returned from the drugstore, excited. From her purse, she pulled out a dark blue spiral notebook. "Praise the Lord and pass the ammunition!" she said, like she'd just scratched off a winning lotto ticket.

She shook the book at the sky like an offering to the gods. "*The Notebook Method of Divorce*!" the Lady said, titling a book she said would be her next big business. "I'm writing everything down so I can sell it. Would you look at these pockets?" She flipped through the card stock.

I sank into my twenty-four-year-old brother's futon. The sunset peeked through the metal mini-blinds as I examined my blue pen. I didn't know what a divorce was, but I could guess. The Lady had made a conscious choice to place our silverware in the trunk. Maybe it was a cold-blooded plan to leave my father behind without cutlery. Or maybe she was going to hawk it. Whatever it was, the stakes were growing as fast as Vermillion County's corn. This was my parents' pattern: growing weary of what they were doing and whom they were doing it with. The mania and depression, the listlessness and hysteria, were all part of the Lady's modus operandi. Self-medicated minds are hard to soothe.

I reached up to my hair. With a twist-pop-pull, a chunk of permed strands fell to the floor.

| SIX |

Southern Shrinking

F OR ALL HIS SCHIZOPHRENIA AND OVER-THE-TOP UN-ruliness, King was, in my six-year-old mind, the more reliable parent. My father's mental unsteadiness was obvious and outward. You could look at him and guess how loud the carnival barkers in his head were. But the Lady's ups and downs were a crapshoot. As soon as I thought I'd nailed it like a game of gin rummy, she switched strategies.

We'd been at Lee's just twenty-four hours when I filled his shower with blood. I'd been washing my hair, but in a new space with my pediatric myopia, I hadn't noticed the Lady's razor, blade side up, on the floor. I sliced my pinkie toe. My first instinct was to scream. But by the time we'd hit the Ohio state border, I'd come to realize that the Lady preferred quiet. From the moment I sank into those velour seats in the new Olds headed for Cincinnati, I was becoming my mother's daughter. I was learning to disappear.

Pain is the brain killer, I thought now.

I pulled my foot to my face and examined my toe. Warm blood ran down my arms.

My brother had given the Lady his bed, where she was now sipping her morning coffee. Lee was already on campus. The Lady's head was propped up on pillows, and she scribbled marginalia for *The Notebook Method of Divorce.*

"Mom!" I called when I couldn't get my toe to stop spurting.

"Oh, for goodness' sakes," she said, peeling herself from the sheets to find me in the tub. "Watch where you're stepping!" She stopped the drain and let the water rise.

"Sit down; let it soak."

It needed a stitch or three, but the inconvenience of dressing sent her back to bed with her notebook.

"I am not a *medical* nurse," she'd told many of her nursing supervisors.

"But you are," they'd said, stunned, tapping their name tags with the initials *RN,* which matched hers.

"I don't do *medical* cases," she'd clarified.

I slumped down in the tub, faint.

"Don't get out till it's done."

By "done," I didn't know if she meant the bleeding or my last breath. It took a good hour to clot.

When Lee examined my prune of a foot that night after clinicals, he told the Lady, "It needed stitches."

The Lady looked on with pride at Lee's diagnosis.

"He's a *medical* doctor," she liked to tell everyone.

With my bandaged toe propped up on Lee's futon, I lay in the dark, defeated by the very weapon King had taught me to wield with ease as a preschooler. Sitting on King's kitchen counter chopping drugs, I wasn't afraid of a silly razor. But that day, Budgie's strength drained from me; remnants of my Indiana life were already as shriveled as my foot.

By the next morning, *The Notebook Method of Divorce* was filled with notes, newspaper clippings, magazine articles, and phone numbers. Lee had the day off, and he and the Lady sat in the warm summer light of his kitchen and planned. My brother would pay for us to move into a Holiday Inn in Chapel Hill, seven miles from him. We'd live on money borrowed from him, running up my only sibling's tab beyond the racks of cash he'd already gifted. They discussed childcare, how to register me for first grade, and a job for Mom.

I sat in a corner and scribbled drawings of two-story houses with windows filled with yellow light and cartoon families, all the time wondering what King was doing without us.

Lee got me dressed and seat-belted into his Honda Civic. We waited for the Lady. She climbed in, and then he drove down the block and dropped me off at a daycare called KinderCare.

"Sorry, Dane," he said, walking me to the door with a red school-bell roof logo. "Mom and I are going to run errands. Then we'll be back for you. Promise."

I walked inside to while away my time in this form of "college," a necessity while my brother and mother met with housing contacts and completed school paperwork. I sat on the red carpet and kept to myself, watching as kids taller and wider than me played with Duplo blocks and trains. I wondered what Lindah and Doggy were doing, whether they were playing Barbies in the Lewman Museum or rummaging through Grandmother's wicker trunk of *Golden Girls* clothes.

I'd disappeared from their lives and our midnight bike rides. Had they even noticed?

At snack time, the KinderCare workers herded us to low tables where boxes of cereal and full gallons of milk awaited us. I was competent at pouring from a Hawaiian Punch can, but a gallon of milk mystified me. I stared as fellow six-year-olds lifted the huge plastic vessels as big as their chests. They poured, and I memorized their technique, watching as boys and girls hoisted them as easily as stuffed animals. I thought about saying I wasn't hungry, but I was. I stepped in line at the last possible minute, too famished to turn away. But when I tried to lift a gallon myself, my arms went limp. My Froot Loops drowned, and my aim failed. Milk overflowed the bowl and spilled onto the table. I dropped the gallon to the hoots of the other six-year-olds.

There, at the KinderCare snack table, I melted into a self-conscious ball of shame. In that moment, I was no longer King's confident razor-blade-wielding Budgie chopping for lip bags. I was the soon-to-be first-grade runt who'd never even touched a gallon of milk. While being a lookout felt natural and danger was exhilarating, I was confounded by practical life skills, the ABC's, polite southern language, and age-appropriate behavior. Beaten by a dairy demon, I'd lost my edge—my Sammy Terry and Vincent Price lessons evaporated. All that remained was a boyish six-year-old who used to know how to wash her hair without stepping on a razor.

That day, I got the message that if I were going to survive North Carolina, I'd need to adapt to the landscape. It was the difference between being my father's daughter and my mother's daughter.

King had been eager to toughen me up with street smarts

that facilitated my Vermillion County survival. "Everyone is your enemy, soldier," he'd said. It was like walking through the world with closed fists.

"One-third of the people you meet won't like you," the Lady said. It was like walking through the world, begging with open palms. Though she was quick to trash-talk and cut people off, the people-pleasing skills that the Lady instilled would facilitate my (and her) southland survival.

I was now of two worlds—Indiana and North Carolina— and I took up a shape-shifting identity to be the daughter they needed in each environment.

But if Vermillion County was my heritage, what could this new world offer me?

I lost those formative years of discovering who I really was, of knowing where my *home* was. It sent me on an incessant quest of looking for myself—for home—in all the wrong places.

After Lee fastened my seatbelt in the Civic that afternoon at the end of my KinderCare nightmare, the Lady turned to the back seat and said, "Your father doesn't want us anymore. I'm flying out to Indiana tomorrow to get our things."

My brother fronted our mother the money for the flight. He promised her that he and his Duke medical school buddies would babysit me in between their hospital clinical rotations. Lee was good on his word, and for the next three days, they fed me McDonald's sundaes and danced with me in the living room to *Solid Gold* Dancers, a choreography game based on the show, which I adapted to go with MTV videos. I outdanced twenty-somethings who panted around the room with me until we all collapsed in giddy exhaustion.

When my mother returned from Indiana, she boasted about her success with King.

"I took your dad out to lunch and told the movers to pack *everything* while we were gone," she said. "Didn't even leave him a pot to pee in." She smiled.

We spent two weeks with Lee, the maximum duration any twenty-four-year-old could house his mother and baby sister without embarrassment. Using one of Uncle Charlie's contacts, the Lady and Lee found housing in Chapel Hill on a bus route to a good elementary school. Lee loaned us money to put down a deposit and rent. Then we moved back into the Holiday Inn to wait for the condo and furniture, my brother paying the bill again.

At the hotel, I left the Lady out of my waitressing games. Instead, I kept to myself, chatting up imaginary customers who filled my invisible apron with cash tips.

Two weeks later, we moved into Brookwood Condos in Chapel Hill, just across from University Place, a mall with anchor department stores at either end. As labeled boxes were unloaded into the two-story, two-bedroom place the Lady couldn't afford, I played outside, exploring more kinds of trees I'd never seen before.

The Lady divided my bunk beds and took one. I combed through boxes until I found the My Little Pony sleeping bag Viper had given me and placed it on my bed.

"You're going to keep that ratty old thing?" she said, as if I had any other treasures.

Mom went across the street to the mall and put expensive furniture on credit cards issued in her own name. Then she installed a custom mirror the size of a wall in my bedroom.

"Pretty is as pretty does," she said. "This is a real fresh start for us!"

I inherited the record player Lee had gifted King and the Lady back at the Indiana trailer. The only record I had was the *Thriller* album, and King had trained me to play Vincent Price's spooky laugh track at the end of the title single.

The next morning, the Lady woke me up with a cup of coffee and a song: "Good morning to you! Good morning to you! We're all in our places with bright, shining faces! This is the way, this is the way to start a new day!"

The sun was barely up, and she sat on the side of my bed topped with the My Little Pony sleeping bag. "Drink this. I don't want you turning out like your dad."

I wiped my eyes and sipped the sweet milky coffee as she explained that we were going on an adventure to a tall office building next to a McDonald's.

"He's *psychotic*," she added as she laid out clothes for me, picking out pink shorts and a frilly white top Grandmother had bought for me. "A real *sociopath*."

I didn't know what the latter meant, but I knew she didn't want the former in her life. Like learning to pour a gallon of milk at KinderCare, I needed to wake up and adapt. The Lady had no use for me if I were sleepy and lazy and sliced by razors and, above all, like my father. If I wasn't the daughter she wanted me to be, I'd be tossed aside like her two husbands and all the "no-goods." It was easier to conform than get the boot. Nothing compared to the nightmare of abandonment by the only parent I had left: I pictured the Lady dropping me off at a fire station like on TV dramas, where exhausted parents relinquished babies they didn't want.

"This is all for you," she said, pulling her worn copy of Tony Robbins's *Unlimited Power* out of her leather purse while we sat on stiff office chairs in a waiting room. "So you won't turn out like your father."

I shifted in my itchy clothes and wished I could have worn my cutoff jeans and *Looney Tunes* T-shirt.

My mother explained that we would be attending weekly therapy sessions with Dr. Gloria. The carrot to get me there was McDonald's, the Lady's attempt to replace Dairy Queen in my favorite food group.

"I love you, but I want other people to *like* you," the Lady said as we waited for our initial meet and greet with Dr. Gloria.

"Remember, Dana, one-third of the people you meet *won't like you*," she said, as if she'd conducted the research herself.

While King taught me to walk through the world seeing everyone as dangerous, the Lady moved through life like everyone had done her wrong. The result was that I became suspicious of everybody—assuming most folks either hated me or were out to kill me. The world, according to my parents, wasn't a friendly place.

At her office, Dr. Gloria interrupted my mother's unverified data dump with a "Nice to meet you!" The Lady gushed over her new therapist and explained how she herself was a psychiatric nurse. "I've had my share of psychotic patients. It's so nice to have someone who understands what it's like dealing with *these* people." The Lady nodded toward me.

I flipped through *Highlights* magazines in Dr. Gloria's waiting room while my mother talked with her behind the closed door.

"Dr. Gloria says I'm a saint!" the Lady said, walking out of her office. "Keeping us afloat like I did."

Dr. Gloria arranged for Dr. Yancy, her clinician husband, to complete a full psychological assessment on me. On our next visit, the Lady and I went to a different waiting room before I was escorted to a room with carpeted baseboards, a constant *whoosh* of industrial air-conditioning, and soft overhead track lighting. It reminded me of the music studios I saw on MTV, where glass walls separated artists from the people who turned voices into synthesizer magic.

For the next few hours, Dr. Yancy administered a variety of tests: Draw-a-Person, Kinetic Family Drawing, Rorschach, Sentence Completion, Tasks of Emotional Development, and the Wechsler Intelligence Scale for Children. It was the kind of intensive analysis that would determine if the Lady's hypothesis about me was right. "You may just be a sociopath like your father," she'd said. "I'm seeing the signs."

But Dr. Yancy disagreed. He met with the Lady to review his findings, which were decidedly healthy but reflective of my home life. Though Mom was confident I had a personality disorder, in his paperwork he declared me a youngster "operating at a superior level of intellectual functioning," but with "post-traumatic stress disorder" and "present emotional resources insufficient to cope with current stressors." According to him, the only intelligence area I didn't excel in was process-oriented tenacity.

"Lazy!" the Lady said. "That's it! I knew it. Just like your father. Haste makes waste, Dana." She smiled because something had been found. I lacked the concentration and stick-to-itiveness required to complete some tasks.

"For your records," the Lady said, handing me a copy of Dr. Yancy's report after they discussed them. I had no idea what I was supposed to do with them, but I noticed that in the margins she'd added her own exposition. Her notes were scribbled in the same hypergraphic style she used in *The Notebook Method of Divorce*. They were the details she felt

Dr. Yancy had overlooked, including that King had abandoned me and that she alone was the one putting up the effort and money to sort me out.

We walked out of the office building, and I squinted in the sunlight. The one thing Dr. Yancy had neglected to uncover was that I was lonely. All the psychological testing in the world couldn't save me from feeling untethered from my father, my Indiana home, my cousins, my aunt and uncle, and my grandparents. Everyone except my mother was gone. My brother was rightfully busy building his own life—the one he deserved. I wasn't schizophrenic or sociopathic or clinically depressed or anxious or whatever else the Lady had been looking for. But Dr. Yancy's findings said that I was traumatized. I was a child who had already accumulated suitcases full of adverse childhood experiences, which, unbeknownst to me, had made me very isolated—and angry.

We went to therapy weekly at Dr. Gloria's office. Over the next five years, we'd spend countless hours in soft fabric chairs, accruing tens of thousands of dollars in debt. While Dr. Gloria prescribed the Lady strong anti-depressants and anti-anxiety pills, my mother was focused on me not "turning out like your father."

"This is costing me a pretty penny," the Lady said on Friday afternoons when she picked me up from Glenwood Elementary School so we could go to therapy.

Those Friday afternoon therapy sessions were our quality time. We got therapy: mental shrinking, analyzing, puréeing, regurgitating. And we ate fast food. I absorbed more coping tools than I realized through play and games with Dr. Gloria. Those afternoons together eased the pinch of lonesomeness, too. But it returned after sundown, when the Lady took an after-dark nap to get ready for the night-nursing job she'd been hired for at Duke University Hospital, where Lee was completing his clinicals.

The Lady was a psychiatric nurse caring for patients with eating disorders. They hid rotting food in holes they cut with contraband knives. The Lady was one of the first nurses to work a Baylor shift, a Texas program started in 1981 to cope with weekend staff shortages. She worked two or three twelve-hour weekend nights in the very same unit where she'd been voluntarily committed in 1968 for three months. It was a joyful homecoming for her.

At work, she was paid a premium to relive her past "vacation" in that unit. When she left for work, babysitters from newspaper want ads were paid twenty-five dollars to spend the night with me. She slept through most of the daylight of the week.

When I went to her bedroom to check in after school, she flipped her wrist like she was shooing a cockroach, blaring the TV news that helped her wake up at five o'clock in the afternoon.

My perceived abandonment was so painful it made my body hurt. I sat on the edge of my bunk bed as it got dark and wrapped myself in Viper's sleeping bag, staring at the mall lights across the street. Fistfuls of my faded perm fell to the beige carpet under my bunk bed, and my trichotillomania worsened. I played with Lee's hand-me-down G.I. Joes and Lindah and Doggy's Barbies and counted the stars on the teddy bear sheets Grandmother had bought me.

Although the Lady left for work at my bedtime and was only ten miles away at Duke, the distance between us could have been measured in galaxies.

But the Lady was in her element. She was surrounded by

therapy, psychiatry, analysis, and powerful prescriptions—her lifelong obsession. My mother loved triage, crisis management, and any patient that made her feel better about the cards life and others had dealt her.

At age six, I didn't know what my mother's issues were. But later I'd discover through the Lady's decades of psychiatric records that her strongest addiction was psychiatry itself. Pages of doctors' notes from her suicide attempts and inpatient hospitalizations insisted that my mother fed off the intellectual aspects of psychology but didn't have the emotional capacity and self-awareness to implement its tools in her own life. According to them, it wasn't entirely her fault: It just wasn't possible. Like many other patients with personality-disorder diagnoses, my mother was missing whatever it is in the brain that allows for recognition and responsibility that leads to change.

The fog around my mother's ailment lifted for me after I turned forty. But not before I'd spent decades carting the Lady to therapy appointments, helping her process her therapy appointments, administering her psych medications, and encouraging her through multiple evidence-based modalities like dialectical behavioral therapy. There was always a program to try and quit, a fellow psych patient who talked too much, or a psychiatrist who didn't know what the hell they were doing. From lithium to Ritalin, manic episodes to paralyzing anxiety, Effexor to Ativan, the Lady moved forward and backward on the gamut of depression-anxiety, all while relishing the smooth high of Lorcet pain pills.

On Sundays in Chapel Hill, because I was home while she worked, the Lady insisted my babysitters trot me over to the church that was a short walk through the mall parking lot. "It will be good for you," she said, recalling the glories of Dr.

Schuller. Binkley Baptist Church had children's programs and Sunday school and was run by a famous minister who'd earned a reputation for social activism by insisting one of his church members, Coach Dean Smith, integrate the UNC men's basketball team. Because of the minister's influence, Coach Smith recruited his first Black athlete.

I never questioned going to church. It had always been an adequate distraction, and I was used to my parents' religious zeal. From Dr. Schuller to TV preachers to Binkley, I didn't balk at faith as a part of life. And like Dr. Gloria's weekly therapy, it made a deeper impression on me than I realized at the time.

I'd begun my first-grade year at Glenwood Elementary School with no word from King. *We'll never see him again,* I told myself. All I had left of him were his lessons that kept me safe. Just as I had on my first drug drop in the backwoods of Indiana, I moved through the hallways and classrooms like a lookout poised to deal with an imminent threat. I distrusted my classmates and teachers. Though I wanted to belong, I opted for a concrete social bunker that shielded me from abandonment. My first school days consisted of bus rides, homework, and the TV headphones the Lady gave me so I could watch afternoon cartoons while she slept. I spent August tiptoeing around our condo so as not to waken her.

By September, the divorce was in full throttle.

"See you in court!" I said to my mother's dentist.

The Lady was sitting in the chair on a rare weekday afternoon out of bed, waiting for an emergency root canal at the cheapest tooth joint in town: our local university's dental school. The twenty-four-year-old dental student looked up from his work, perplexed at a first-grader threatening litigation.

"I'm getting a divorce; we've been spending a lot of time at the lawyer's office," Mom mumbled, mouth full of cotton.

In addition to our visits to Dr. Gloria, the Lady schlepped me to dentists and lawyers on those afternoons. I learned to navigate a waiting room like a champ, straightening stacks of *Time* and *Sports Illustrated*. While other kids played with baskets of toys in corners or threw tantrums, I cleaned and organized like Santa's elf, quietly making myself useful and absorbing office jargon.

"She's such a good helper!" the Lady would say as receptionists wondered at my inability to be a child.

While my adulting was unmatched, my hair pulling was getting worse.

Dr. Gloria's bills piled up, as did invoices from the bulldog lawyers, which the Lady placed on her credit card.

"Put it on my tab," she told them with a smile. "I'll squeeze him for every dime."

But it was a futile, debt-accruing endeavor to milk a man who only dealt in dime bags. King's cash business had gotten the best of her. King balked at garnering assets. His constitution was averse to owning anything of value—having to care for it and repair it, instead of trashing it and moving on. My father lived out a staunch financial philosophy of "don't fence me in," inhabiting a world in which you could dust the dirt off your calloused feet and flee. He lived by the rule that all you needed was a trailer with a reliable hitch. And if that happened to slip through your Vaseline-greased palms, there was always a hearse to be had. Phone lines, mortgages, and papers were for idiots, my father would say. He had no official trail of property assets or wages. Later, King wouldn't even have the forty quarters of work he would need to collect social security.

"Cah-yeesh," King liked to repeat in his distinct Vermillion County vernacular, which included words like "Tuesdee," "Weds-dee," "skoo-ul," and "poo-ul." He lived for the crumpled bills he slammed on Walmart counters and the bands he pulled from kiddie-ride boxes. Credit cards could be traced; worse yet, he taught me, they led to delusions of luxury, which led to debt, which led to bankruptcy, as the Lady would later find out.

King said cash was blunt: It barked your real worth. And the Lady and I were broke.

SEVEN

King, Unhinged

ON FRIDAYS, THE LADY AND I ATE AT MCDONALD'S on spare change, and I played Life under Dr. Gloria's direction. At home, my sadness turned to fuming, as I assumed that King's silence meant he was spurning me as well as my mother. Why hadn't my father fought for me? Why hadn't he gotten a job to pay for a phone line so that he could at least call me? I coped with my loneliness and anger at King's apparent rejection by dancing furiously in the living room to Madonna tapes blaring from the cassette player Lee had given my parents the Christmas before we left with the silverware in the trunk. I could find happiness only through movement—dancing and walking—which proved to be annoying to my mother. "Can't you just sit still?" the Lady said often.

I continued to pull my hair out by the roots and talked with imaginary friends in the woods behind our condo. The Lady gave up on perms and kept my hair cut short in a Dorothy Hamill hairstyle, my brown bowl of tresses thinning by the week. The condo remained under a no-noise policy; daylight was for sleeping. Between her Baylor shifts and my excommunication from her bedroom because of my fidgeting, we hardly saw each other, save for Friday afternoons at therapy. I suspect now that it may have been the way she wanted it. She blamed her unconscious weekdays on old age and menopause. Until I reached an age where I could be still, polite, self-aware, useful, and adult-ish, I was to stay silent and out of her way.

After we left that summer, King disconnected the phone at the Ninth Street trailer. Come late fall, he began making long-distance calls from G&GL's house once he'd stolen another vehicle and gotten enough gas money to drive to Dana. The first time I heard directly from him, Grandmother initiated the call and worked it out with the Lady, who succumbed to the sternness Grandmother used when she was adamant.

"Budge, it's Dad," King said after I got on the line, as if I'd have forgotten what his voice sounded like. "Long time, no talk, good buddy."

He asked about school and if I was behaving for my mother. I asked when I'd be able to see him. His hoarse voice cracked a little when he said "Soon." King asked if I remembered our midnight bike rides and cozy tuck-ins in the Ninth Street trailer. He updated me on Lindah's and Doggy's Halloween costumes and the changing leaves in Vermillion County. Fall was his favorite season in Dana. The maple tree where Tiger had hung was shedding its bright leaves like snowflakes, and the wind coming off the flatland had already picked up, King said. He didn't mention drug drops or kiddie rides or Viper or Carnival Captivations. I wondered how the business was going without me.

"Meatsweat loves the circus," he said, then coughed a smoker's loogie into his handkerchief. "He'll be gone awhile."

From G&GL's, King planned to drive to North Carolina to pick me up for Christmas. I wasn't certain when or how or even if he'd manage to get to me, but I was excited. I crossed the days off the calendar.

King showed up as soon as Glenwood Elementary School closed for Christmas break, like he'd woken that morning, taken a bump of coke, gotten in the light blue Lincoln he'd lifted from some unsuspecting octogenarian, and driven straight through till he got to me.

He came with gifts. Real diamond earrings and a cubic zirconia ring, a wagon with walkie-talkies, a Barbie house, cash for shopping, and a Doberman pinscher named Stinger. The dog, three times as big as I was, had ridden clear from Indiana to North Carolina in that Lincoln. King tried to teach me how to walk her around our Brookwood complex. But Stinger pulled me to the asphalt and skinned my knees. I screamed.

"Tighten the leash, Budge. Show that bitch who's in charge!" he yelled.

By the day we were to return to Indiana, Stinger had chewed up the Lady's shoes and my brand-new Barbies. King had worn out his welcome, too, making a fire in the condo's fireplace by sawing up the lumber the Lady had purchased to line our flower bed out back. She seemed relieved we were leaving.

We all said goodbye again, this time in the blacktop parking lot of our condo complex. Now, months after that first somber *so long* in the Ninth Street gravel driveway, my stomach twisted in the hope that things would somehow return to the way they had been. But I felt the difference now, like a fluorescent light had been flipped on, casting a harsh purple glow on reality. These were now two different parents on very different turf.

When I was in North Carolina, I was the Lady's daughter. As I was indoctrinated by her new vocabulary of *psychotic, manic-depressive, custody battles,* and *sociopath* and *root canals,* any remaining crumbs of childhood were swept into the dustbin and tossed out. On her turf, King's mannerisms, street smarts, illicit business, and aggressive surprise guard dogs were loud, outrageous, and embarrassing. When I was on King's turf, being raised as his Vermillion County daughter, I saw him as another person: tough and quirky—but capable.

Their antipodal parenting and personalities confounded me. King's avoidance of norms, manners, quiet, therapy, and prescription drugs stood in stark contrast to the Lady's overindulgence in all of them.

It was the summer in reverse, now having to say goodbye to the Lady in the cold of winter. I got in the Lincoln, and we pulled out of the parking lot on shocks as smooth as a glassy-topped pond.

Even though I'd crossed off the days until King would come to pick me up and take me home, still I felt uneasy. For the first time since we'd left Vermillion County, I ached to stay with my mother. It was the same feeling I'd had on that new-moon night when we hit the deer and Viper took the gun.

"Just like old times, Budgie," King said as we merged onto the interstate, driving away from my mother.

I feigned a smile.

But it wasn't like old times. Now I had questions I was too afraid to ask: Why hadn't I heard from him for so long? Why had he left us in that credit card lurch? Why had the Lady called him psychotic and a sociopath?

He seemed to read my mind. "Just between you and me, your mom's a little uptight. But we're on a tight schedule," he said, the corners of his mouth drawn down. "Just like old times."

The black-market radar Fuzzbuster suction-cupped to the Lincoln's dashboard screeched with high-pitched alerts when cops were nearby.

"Copper got 'em one!" King said. "Bet that no-good son of a bitch is just over this hill." We passed a plain wrapper Crown Victoria. "Cocksucking pig!" he shouted as the state trooper stepped out of the vehicle in a wide-brimmed hat. King lit a joint from the fiery ring of the car lighter, as if I'd forgotten how to work it.

"Cocksucking pig!" I parroted.

"Good Budgie." He patted me on the head. I was happy to regain his affection. The Fuzzbuster resumed its flatline beeps like the hospital machines that tell people in movies when someone is dying.

"Now ball your fist like this, see." King took a toke off the lit joint, then demonstrated a knuckle-sandwich punch and lifted his middle finger like he was pushing an invisible penny heavenward.

As soon as an eighteen-wheeler passed us, he looked the driver in the eye and flipped him off with a "Fuck you, butt boy!"

"Now you try," he said.

The new job was simple: Instead of lighting his joints and tuning the radio, I pressed my paw to the window and gave truckers a knuckle-sandwich penny pusher as we glided by on the left. I didn't know what it meant, but I loved how weathered semi drivers with faded anchor tattoos drew back from their own window in confusion, the way I did when I got my letters mixed up.

"Good job, Budge!" King shouted over my head.

It was the same hubris my father had displayed in hitting the deer and driving on without slowing down for a second. It was the same egotism seen in my mother's decision to wreck Viper's truck at the snowy Canadian border. The idea that we could piss off a semi driver and live to tell the tale—driving away unscathed in our smooth-riding Lincoln—showed an arrogance I'd never encountered in any adults other than my own parents.

Years later, it occurred to me that these antics may well have been signals to truckers that we were riding loaded, trunk full of drugs, so that they could spread the word on their CB radios. When we pulled over at truck stops, I was the lookout again, keeping my distance and my eyes open, as King peddled dope out of the back of the car and taught me how to spy a lot lizard (prostitute).

We drove straight through to Indiana on speed and candy, pulling into the Ninth Street trailer just before Christmas. But the home I'd spent my earliest years in was beyond recognition or repair.

The way the Lady told it, King had quickly moved on without us—his arms around a thriving business and maybe even a new family. I'd imagined that the place the three of us had shared would now be warm and full of food with this replacement family, including a kid who was sharper and quicker and better at cutting drugs than I was. I'd shored myself up to meet a tougher, grittier child now living in my bedroom, driving stolen cars and shanking undesirables like Boozy Piddler. This imaginary first grader had unparalleled prowess in street brawls and a nose for good weed.

But though the Lady had told me "Peter Pan" was having the partying time of his life without us, that wasn't the picture I saw when we arrived.

Instead, it was clear my father had been losing his mind.

After we left that June with the silverware, King dabbled in a full-on Orthodox rabbi costume and persona, trading his farmer overalls and Lakers ball cap for black three-piece suits, even in the middle of a hot summer day. He quoted Levitical law and showed up at his good buddies' homes in taxis with tens of thousands of dollars duct-taped to his chest. He told them he'd just landed in Indianapolis after participating in global trafficking schemes. The feds were after him, he always said, and he'd grown accustomed to sleeping in the cornfields across from the Ninth Street trailer, using the rat-recliner-covered manhole only at dusk and dawn.

When I walked into the trailer that Christmas, the place was trashed. Ceiling tiles were razored and the carpet was sliced up. All that remained of our life together was my parents' mattress—the only thing the Lady had left King—which was a rectangular heap of springs under a quarter-inch of soiled nylon. He'd pulled out the stuffing so the government couldn't hide their bugs, King told me. My father even cut off the back bedroom that had once held the present-day equivalent of six figures' worth of 1980s drug inventory behind the mirrored closet doors. He'd literally and metaphorically sealed the door to the space he and the Lady had shared—where she'd guarded the heart and soul of Carnival Captivations—from the rest of the trailer.

Though King had flashed gifts and cash and a thorough-bred dog when he picked me up in Chapel Hill, the trailer was barren. The cozy light over the stove was burned out. The Indiana winter wind whipped up through the trapdoor and down through the ravaged ceiling. Even King's living room, once full of couches and disciples and blaring TV preachers, was empty and quiet. The moldy refrigerator didn't even have the ingredients for our ketchup sandwiches.

According to the Lady, King was psychotic. In a way, she was right.

I was putting together what the word meant. When I put down my duffel bag on the dirty carpet of my old bedroom, it was Christmas Eve.

"Time to go to the Walmarts!" King said, wide eyed. "This is a big sacrifice, Budge, just so you know." After he pulled some cash from the water heater, we piled back into the Lincoln. I felt the same loneliness as when the Lady left and went to work at night, even though I was in King's presence now.

At Walmart, King stationed me in the toy aisle and told me to pick whatever I wanted. The word *sacrifice* had thrown me off in the same way as when the Lady complained about the money she was spending on therapy, so I picked only a red camping canteen to hold my chocolate milk.

But instead of letting me use it when we got home, King took the bag and the gift. It reappeared the next morning, propped against the wood-paneled wall with a note saying it was from Santa.

"Got your chocolate milk, Budge!" King said when I un-wrapped the canteen. Thankfully, G&GL had us over for Christmas dinner. We arrived later that morning to the warmth of Grandmother's kitchen and the smell of simmering food. Aunt Marietta and Uncle Leuge showered me with gifts and love.

"Glad you're home, honey," Uncle Leuge said when he hugged me tight. Aunt Marietta wiped away her tears. "Love you, kiddo," she said. Lindah and Doggy shared their Santa toys with me, and the three of us pretended like I'd never left. It made me want to stay forever.

But instead, the morning after Christmas, I woke up in the trashed trailer. King and I climbed into the Lincoln, and we went out and rented two VCRs from the Clinton video store down by the Wabash River. He slapped sweaty bills on the counter in exchange for the machinery and unmarked VHS cases that were as shiny as library books. Lee had given the Lady and King a VCR one Christmas before their divorce, but the Lady had swiped it the day she had the movers load up the truck.

"Pick a movie, Budge, any movie," King instructed.

I chose one called *Legend*, which had Tom Cruise on the plastic sleeve, only because I recognized his face from *The Color of Money*.

King handed me our stack of movies and tucked the VHS players under his arm. When we got home, he moved the trapdoor chair from above the manhole so that I could sit in front of the TV.

"Keep these closed," King said, pulling the polyester curtains tight across the trailer's plastic windows. "It's too cold."

"Look! Microscope eyes!" I said to King, showing off how close I could get to the TV.

"You'll ruin your eyes," he fussed. "Milk's in the fridge."

By first grade, my vision had become as blurry as a dirty

window. After I stepped on the razor blade, the Lady took me to the eye doctor for heavy plastic frames and thick lenses in the style of grandmas who play canasta.

King retreated to my old bedroom, now filled with what remained of his mattress, pushed up against the wall. The room was dimly lit by a lamp he'd stolen, and the beige plastic door-knob had been removed. A hole the size of a silver dollar remained in the door, just big enough to peer inside the room.

I watched *Legend* three times before I got bored, hitting the pause button to refill my chocolate milk and pee. I felt my way down the hall to the bathroom by the closed back bedroom where I used to visit the Lady.

When I passed my old room, I peeked through the hole and called out to King. He shouted at me not to bother him and to keep watching my Tom Cruise movie. I retreated to the living room and sat in the rat-recliner, watching *Legend* two more times. By then I was starving.

I went down the hall and looked through the hole again. "I'm hungry," I told King. I was used to entertaining and feeding myself while the Lady worked Baylor shifts, but his fridge was empty.

"Get away from there!" King said.

Through the hole, I saw King sprawled out on the mattress, a dirty Fruit of the Loom shirt covering his chest. I didn't understand what he was doing with himself, but I looked across the room and saw a woman's body thrashing about on the TV.

I moved away from the hole and rested my back on the wood paneling in the hallway. I slid down to the dirty carpet. King didn't say another word, and he didn't come out of the bedroom. I went back into the living room for another round of *Legend*, hoping he would finish whatever he was doing and take me to Dairy Queen or G&GL's for brown cows. It had been more than eight hours at this point, which I knew only because we'd started out at the movie store in the morning and it was now pitch dark.

When King finally emerged from my old room, he said, "Budge, get in here." I flipped off *Legend* and ran down the hall.

The door was open and the TV was off. King had on his overalls over a well-worn white shirt.

Before we moved to North Carolina, the Lady and I used to fight over King's undershirts, washed to death, cotton turned to silk. Their softness felt like being wrapped in a warm hug; we competed to see who could get to one first. King wore them with no underwear, stretching the shirts over his genitals like cotton hammocks, feigning modesty.

"Match 'em up, kid," King said, pointing to the heap of VHS plastic on the floor of my old room. "Put them tapes back in their right covers."

It was an alphabetical challenge for a slow-reading kid who, according to Dr. Yancy, lacked tenacity.

Debbie Does Dallas. "A. B. C. D," I mumbled to myself. "*D* is the fourth letter of the alphabet. Look for another *D. D* as in *Dana.*" *Nymphs' Naughty Nights.* "*N. N* as in *North Carolina.*"

It took me thirty minutes to match six tapes to their rightful cases.

"Hurry it up, kid!" King said. We slid into the Lincoln. "I'll show you a porno one day. Best way to learn."

I nodded.

Like the Lady's *psychotic* and *sociopath,* the word *porno* evaded my elementary school vocabulary. I found out years later that Grandmother had called the Lady that day—the

Legend day—and expressed her concern. Though he was a devil to her, she was loyal to her son, but she wasn't happy that King said that he and I were sharing the mattress in that bedroom. The Lady dismissed Grandmother's concern, a strange move for a woman who insisted that King was crazier than a bedbug.

When she got nowhere with my mother, Grandmother called King on the landline she had installed and paid for just for my visit, insisting that I come stay the remainder of the break with them and spend time with Lindah and Doggy. I wanted to go. It was a golden ticket to escape movies on repeat and the trashed trailer and no food and strange peephole shows.

But King was adamant that I stay. "You're not going. That's final, young lady," he said and hung up.

"Please, Dad—I'll never ask for anything else again, ever. Promise," I begged. I longed for Grandmother's brown cows and the warm tumbling sound of Aunt Marietta's dryer (or anyone's dryer) and food.

"Please, please, please," I said.

King's narrowed eyes met mine. He lowered himself to my level and snarled the nastiest words I'd ever heard him speak: "If you go, I'll kill myself! I'll kill myself. Do you fucking understand that, Dana?

"I'll kill myself! I'll kill myself! I'll kill myself!" He shouted it over and over like a mantra, raging around the trashed trailer like a Molotov cocktail threatening to light up the room and everything in it.

Instead of letting loose my own explosion, as I'd been trained to do in the face of terror and horror and danger, I froze. I closed my eyes and tilted my chin to my chest, quiet.

King's anger turned to groveling. He slumped to his knees and bawled at my feet, pawing at me like a toddler who believes that his parent is saying goodbye forever. "Don't go. Don't go," he pleaded, crying. "If you go, then I'll kill myself."

If I leave him, he will die. It will be my fault.

"I'm staying. I'm staying. I'm staying," I whispered.

"Great!" he said and popped to his feet. He laughed, skipped to my old bedroom, and closed the door.

PART II

Tough times never last, but tough people do!

—Dr. Robert Schuller

EIGHT

North Carolina Is My Home

I T'S HARD TO CONVEY THE CHASM THAT THE *LEGEND* DAY
and King's suicide threat broke open in my life. His schizophrenia, already heightened when we left, was intensified
by his incessant drug use. Squeezed as if in a vise, my father's
brain was incapable of making better decisions.

By age six, I already felt disjointed and disassociated, like
I didn't belong to myself or my body. *My brain is on fire,* I'd
tell myself, trying to parse why my mind was frenetic and
anxious, like a room of walkie-talkies competing for a blue
ribbon in racket-making.

The fallout from King's actual psychosis—his nervous
breakdown, his suicide threats, his porn addiction—ripped
through my childhood like a maul that splits dried wood.
When he drove me back to North Carolina after Christmas, I
was changed. Quiet. Withdrawn. Turned inward.

By New Year's, I was despondent and sullen, but I didn't
know how to verbalize all the harrowing things that had hap-

pened with King over Christmas break. When Dr. Gloria and the Lady saw my newfound meanness and doldrums, they suspected I was going through typical kid tantrums. I didn't say anything other than to tell Mom I didn't want to go back to Vermillion County. She was giddy.

I gravitated toward the more "stable" of my parents—like how Grandfather's Battle of the Bulge grenade left him eight-fingered but alive, I was trying to choose the grenade that would sever one limb instead of all four.

King's "veeshun" of my Vermillion County inheritance evaporated. Long gone were my (and his) dreams that I'd become his tough Carnival Captivations business partner, growing in acumen with age, perfecting my lookout and drop skills, hustling grown men out of bands of cash. Instead, I made myself as useful as the silverware in the Lady's trunk. Sturdy. Dependable. Helpful.

I would need to hide those formative Indiana years and their illicit associations. If I became an Indiana denier, I reasoned, my years there could be erased like an expunged record. *A fresh start never hurt anyone,* I told myself. Toys and memories could be replaced. Many kids did okay without one parent, like living with a solo kidney. If I were to survive the polite southern culture of North Carolina—and my mother's personality disorders—I needed to regroup.

King's and the Lady's diametric parenting styles were confusing, but one parent had now jumped meters ahead toward abuse, and my brain alerted me like I was on a drug drop gone wrong. King's criminal training, though not safe, had never felt abusive. The destroyed trailer, the paranoia, the neglect, the porn, the mattress sharing, and the suicide threat *did.*

I was forced to serve the Lady full time and cater to her personality disorders, which, though not healthy, didn't result in razored ceilings, dark trailers, hunger, and suicide threats that took my child brain to its breaking point. The Lady's brand of mental illness was more insidious than physically dangerous.

So, at age six, I found myself hundreds of miles from Vermillion County and from the father I adored—who was now sick beyond recognition. I was forced to leave behind my namesake and King's prophecies. Now my drug-drop training and Hoosier lessons were as useless in North Carolina as the Lady's *Notebook Method of Divorce.*

But more than that, I was coping with the sudden death of a parent who wasn't even dead.

"Survival mode" was what the Lady called those elementary school years. "We just have to stand on our heads, that's all," she said.

Mental gymnastics was the game she played anytime she faced an obstacle. She would scribble minutes on a yellow legal pad in quarter-hour increments, then tick them off with tally marks like an addict taking it breath by breath.

After he graduated from Duke when I was eight, Lee moved back to Ohio to complete a family-medicine residency. The Duke eating-disorder unit where Mom worked closed. She was offered a transfer to one of the hospital's gastrointestinal units. She refused. "I don't do medical cases," she barked when they described the job with its high pay and weekday hours.

" 'No, thank you,' I told them. 'I do *not* care for *that.*' Who do they think I am, anyway? I'm not taking care of patients after they've had abdominal surgery. That's *dirty* work."

A series of ill-fated, short-term nursing jobs ensued over the next two years. No one matched her Duke Baylor shift paycheck. The Lady slept while she paid a journalist to cook up an expensive-looking résumé on oatmeal-colored paper. It landed her a research job at the University of North Carolina at Chapel Hill. That position went off the rails as soon as it began, with verbal disputes with co-workers and workers' comp injuries. Her eventual firing was cloaked as a layoff.

Meanwhile, weekly therapy with Dr. Gloria continued. And the bills kept piling up.

"I'm not paying her to play board games with you," the Lady announced one Friday after my session. McDonald's treats and mother-daughter therapy time were dumped for unemployment-office woes and credit card minimum payments. By the spring I turned eleven, we'd spent five years in weekly therapy. Tens of thousands of dollars later, I still wasn't as fixed as the Lady wanted.

I stuffed my pain like I was packing a kiddie-ride cardboard box with kilos and kept pulling out fistfuls of hair and having solo dance parties in the living room. The Lady had begun to tolerate both only because she bought herself a Walkman. She traded in *The 700 Club* for Tony Robbins's 1989 *Personal Power!* tapes. Lee bought me an Apple IIGS computer, and I played the *Reader Rabbit* game after school. He paid for encyclopedias and encouraged me to read and write stories on the computer. I thumbed through the heavy red-spined books and read about religious iconography and mysteries, travel and ancient languages.

School wasn't all bad. Glenwood Elementary was full of kids whose parents were finishing up PhDs at local universities. As much as I wanted to hate my classmates, they were creative and open-minded. Even the ones I'd rejected before they could discard me invited me to their birthday parties.

Teachers tried extra hard too. My fifth-grade teacher, Mr. Slaydon, had a brown ponytail and played guitar. When I told him I liked writing stories, he moved me into a special cohort of eleven-year-olds who wrote scripts and shot them on heavy video cameras paid for with a grant.

The only words I heard from King in those years were through letters written in frenzied script. They were as indecipherable as his 1960s military letters during the hot-box period, with underlines and highlights and references to "the last years of my life." Once, King sent a Valentine's "I Heart U" treat. The block letters *I* and *U* hugged a heart of chocolate as big as my fist. I wouldn't open it. Instead, I put it in the refrigerator for safekeeping. I saw the sugary message only through its clear plastic, observing the guarded treasure each time I opened the door.

In the spring of 1992, the dogwoods had just begun to bud when the Lady hung up the phone with her brother, who had begged her not to declare bankruptcy. She said, "This is all your father's fault. He's ruined us."

Even though she'd earned upwards of fifty thousand dollars a year in the 1980s from her Duke Baylor shift, the Lady's credit lines had run out. She'd failed in handling her personal finances.

Lee now lived in Maryland and helped cover our basics—food and rent—with his doctor job while our mother buckled in for bankruptcy court. My brother and his wife used time off to drive down and move us to a cheaper apartment in Glen Lennox, less than two miles from Brookwood. We could stay for three months until we found a place to land. What was supposed to be a fresh start in Chapel Hill was now a dead end.

During the bankruptcy proceedings, the Lady's scalp began to bleed. It was a strange phenomenon caused by stress from all the bills. She dabbed her thin skin and frosted blond hair with orange Merthiolate, a poisonous antiseptic containing mercury. Dried blood coated her typically pristine fingernails.

Not long after that phone call with her brother, she announced that she'd made "an executive decision." "We're moving to Reidsville. Mother needs us. Your aunts and uncles have made a mess of things."

Reidsville, North Carolina, was her hometown. The Lady's four siblings were navigating my maternal grandmother's Alzheimer's diagnosis. They had it under control, they said. But the Lady was leveraging her mother's illness to run from the larger crisis: the bankruptcy that would take her credit cards away for seven years and force relatives to be her bank account co-signers.

Just like she had when she clutched at Viper's farmhouse plan, the Lady fluttered about like a hummingbird, invigorated by her mother's dimming memory and our upcoming move.

Then in June on my last day at Glenwood Elementary School, she made another executive decision: "You're going to church camp. Period." She gave me a look as if to say, *No ifs, ands, or buts.*

I sulked for days in anticipation of our separation. I'd grown attached to her in a way that flipped our roles. I was concerned about how she would do without me. We didn't necessarily spend a lot of time together in those elementary school years, but at home I could keep an eye on her.

At Montreat Conference Center in the mountains of

western North Carolina, I made tearful calls back home to the Lady. As our chaperone, the Binkley church camp minister, waved me toward activities, I glued myself to the pay phone and begged my mother to come pick me up. Our move that summer to Reidsville would be the fifth in my eleven years, and I was going to be stuck at church camp while it was happening.

From Los Angeles to Vermillion County to temporary housing in motels to Lee's apartment to Brookwood to Glen Lennox and now to my mother's hometown, I'd never once had the luxury of a goodbye. Now my feeling of disorientation was heightened with the thought that, for the second time in a year, my life was being uprooted without my being there. Movers had packed up my Ninth Street trailer bedroom without me, and they were going to do the same at our Glen Lennox apartment.

After the move to Reidsville, my mother's brothers arranged for us to live rent-free for six months in one of their two-story, three-bedroom Chatmoss apartments. Though she was excited, still the Lady was reluctant to crawl back to her hometown, just as she and King had timidly coasted back to Indiana on borrowed gas money three months after I was born.

Back then, we'd lived in Boot's trailer in G&GL's front yard. It was a new low for King to take charity from the baby brother he hated more than the devil. Boot, in turn, relished holding something over his eldest brother. Living in Boot's place was the impetus my parents needed to put the brand-new Ninth Street trailer on credit, before King threatened to kill Boot a second time. Eleven years later, the Lady and I were back where we started, mooching off a sibling's largesse.

Chatmoss Apartments were twenty-some brick units on Reidsville's Main Street. Within walking distance of the YMCA, First Baptist Church, Family Dollar, and the hospital, they stood out as an eyesore among well-kept buildings and the Italianate and Queen Anne mansions that still stood on Main Street, a holdover from before the railroad and the town's industrialization settled in.

The first night we spent in the apartment, I was awakened by our burly next-door neighbor arriving home at midnight. I watched from my bedroom window as he poured himself from the passenger side door and vomited drunk chunks onto the ground. Then he wiped his salt-and-pepper goatee while his designated driver cackled. Five years prior, I would have opened the carriage knife King had given me in preparation for shanking him, following King's instructions to engage and explode. But now, at age eleven, I was withered and worthless, anxious for the sun to rise and burn away the image of a stranger retching beneath the streetlights.

"Rise and shine, and give God the glory, glory!" the Lady sang to me the next morning as I lay in my bunk bed. She'd brought me a brown-speckled mug of coffee with milk and sugar. "Blessed beyond measure," she whispered.

I sat up.

"Praise God we are here, Dana."

She hadn't spouted this much God language since we'd left the Ninth Street trailer and she'd traded in Tammy Faye and Dr. Schuller for Tony Robbins. Besides, it was King who'd been the Vermillion County cult leader, with his "veeshuns," his "Precious Jesus!" his insistence on our Jewish heritage, even his superglued crucifixes on stolen dashboards.

"We're going to church today, little girl!" the Lady said.

"Got a lot to be thankful for!" Besides some visits to the Baptist church in Chapel Hill, we hadn't been to worship together much during my elementary school years.

"Time to get dressed and act like you're somebody." She scurried around my ten-by-ten wood-paneled room, digging in boxes for my baptism dress. She laid out a slip and pantyhose. "Appearances *matter*. This is all we've got!"

The Lady's middle brother, Uncle Elton, and his wife, Aunt Plum, picked us up in their new-smelling car with leather seats to drive us the half mile to First Baptist Church on Main Street, where my mother and all her siblings had been baptized and raised in the Southern Baptist faith. At the door of the sanctuary, the Lady adjusted my showing slip and smoothed my caterpillar eyebrows with her spit.

We sat in "the Trent family pew" not twenty feet from the elevated pulpit. I kept quiet and followed the bulletin's directions. Dr. Allan, the pastor, cued Jesus hymns and preached with a kindness akin to Dr. Schuller's softer moments. Church folk offered a cheerful "Welcome back!" to my mother, connecting her with her sibling and her now very sick mother. After more than thirty years away from this place, the Lady was still the small-town beauty queen that people remembered: Evelyn Trent's baby daughter.

After church, Uncle Elton and Aunt Plum took us to Sanitary Café, a homestyle hole-in-the-wall restaurant like something you'd see in Vermillion County. Rusted gas station signs hung from dingy plaster, and aging waitresses kept pencils behind their ears. Salty green beans and buttery mashed potatoes were slopped onto plates from the five-gallon pots in the kitchen. I examined the menu prices and ordered a single bowl of mac 'n' cheese.

"You go on and get whatever you'd like," Aunt Plum interrupted. "Make hers a vegetable *plate*," she told the waitress, "and bring her the biggest bowl of biscuits you've got."

"And you," she said, pointing her diamond-ringed fingers at me, "save room for dessert!"

I cleaned my plate and slouched with a full belly while the adults talked business. My aunt discussed co-signing a bank account for my mother, while my uncle was concerned that I get registered at Reidsville Middle School.

Like Lee, G&GL, Aunt Marietta, and Uncle Leuge had, it was commonplace now for me to see adults who weren't my parents caring for me and making parental decisions, acts that made me feel a measure of safety.

"Our angels," the Lady said when Uncle Elton and Aunt Plum dropped us off at home after lunch. My mother stacked the charity checks from them and friends, along with canned food, in our Chatmoss kitchen.

"He ruined us, you know," she said as she stripped down to her full slip for a nap. "Your father never paid one dime of child support for you. I've been running this show on my own. It's not easy being a single parent, you know."

I nodded. "Thanks, Mom. I appreciate all you do for me."

"You're quite welcome, young lady. Couldn't have you turning out like that sociopath. But it was a close call. Gloria's not happy with us," she said.

Dr. Gloria, along with a list of other Chapel Hill attorneys and doctors and apartment complexes, had been named in the bankruptcy claim.

"Remember, the world owes you nothing; you owe the world *everything*," she said.

By "world," I knew she meant *her*.

"Take a nap. We'll be back at church for vespers tonight," she said.

I dutifully lay down on the bunk bed in my Chatmoss bedroom.

The First Baptist Church Sunday-Wednesday rhythm anchored our weeks. "We'll be here any time the doors are open!" the Lady bragged to the pastor.

At home, she reminded me, "It's free."

I attended Sunday school, children's choir, Bible study, and other church activities. Church was not nearly as excruciating as it had been with King around.

"Pharisee!" he'd say from the parking lot or the pew. He'd been raised at Dana Community Bible Church, but he fancied himself in charge of his own kind of religion. And it was the kind of religion that let him watch preachers on cable while smoking a doobie.

I didn't tell anyone at First Baptist Church about King or Vermillion County or Carnival Captivations. I knew that if I started a conversation by asking other people questions and proved I was a good listener who remembered names and details, they'd talk about themselves all day long. Dale Carnegie taught me that skill the first time the Lady made me read *How to Win Friends and Influence People*. Besides, it was my chance to start fresh and be curious about other people. A new church in a new town was an opportunity for reinvention. No need to bother anyone with details like kiddie-ride drug trafficking and psychological tests for schizophrenia. I didn't mention Chapel Hill or Dr. Gloria or even that I had a father.

"Such good manners," the gray-haired church folks would tell Mom.

But my teachers felt differently.

"You're a fireball, aren't you?" Principal Ross said to me the first week of sixth grade.

Reidsville Middle School looked like the county jail where the Lady had taken a weekend nursing job. Every Saturday, I made the trek with her to an actual jail in the county seat, where men in brown sheriff uniforms watched men watching cable TV on closed-circuit cameras.

"Keeps them from killing each other," a sheriff's deputy told me.

The teachers who made middle schoolers watch *Channel One News* with Anderson Cooper said the same thing about us.

But Reidsville Middle School was a hotbed of junior-high hormones and cliques and haves and have-nots. The Dale Carnegie social strategies that worked on octogenarians at church fell flat at school, and I fell to the bottom of every barrel, the new kid no one wanted to sit by or talk to. The only middle schooler who surpassed me in strangeness was George. Students made fun of him for his old-man name, and when he tried to befriend me—the other outcast—out of pity, no amount of TV could quell my anger, which brimmed over like the stringy southern Brunswick stew I was learning to eat. I didn't want to be associated with losers, though I was one.

Principal Ross called me to his office after I busted George's lip. "Yep. Fireball. I can see it," he said, squinting through wire-rimmed glasses. "You keep those fists to yourself, young lady."

"Yes, sir," I said, slouched down in his scratchy red chair, a far cry from the large monster I'd made myself when I swung at George.

"Get back to class," he said.

Principal Ross never told the Lady about the fight. I took it as a wake-up call. He'd given me another shot, and I'd better not mess it up. Otherwise, my overdrawn emotional bank account with the Lady would land me right in the orphanage.

The Lady got her own wake-up call too. With no credit cards, we had only the money in her checking account to live on. For the first time in her life, she was consistent in both her weekend work at the jail and her weekday work at a public health department. There was no plastic credit card to over-rely on.

"It's the only game in town," she said of her stale nursing jobs while reading a copy of *The Reidsville Review* each morning at six o'clock. She was fifty-two and starting over, listening to the *Out of Africa* soundtrack and wondering what had happened to her life.

The bus dropped me off last after school, which meant an hour's ride through Reidsville's poor Black neighborhoods of rented crumbling houses and poor white neighborhoods of rented rickety trailers. After one week of the route, I'd memorized where everyone lived. Each in their own silo, all the Reidsville kids were convinced they had it the worst and resented all the other kids for it. But poor kids who *look* different have more in common than our parents tell us. We all had distressed lives: tired parents, broke parents, absent parents, drunk parents, strung-out parents, or child-beating parents. And the kids who didn't have parent problems had households with wild siblings and unpaid light bills and empty fridges.

Being able to observe their problems made me think I had none. Sure, my parents were moody, depressed, anxious, volatile, and unregulated, but they never beat me. Food was never too far out of reach; the safety net of well-to-do grand-parents and my older brother ensured we had shelter. I had Aunt Marietta and Uncle Leuge's Indiana caregiving, Uncle Elton and Uncle Charlie's Chatmoss apartment, and Aunt Plum's insistence on full plates at the Sanitary Café. My other two aunts, Ann and Gail, arranged respite sleepovers. Angels were always a call away. And they looked out for me and did things for me I didn't even know about until I was an adult. As long as my body was in motion those elementary and middle school years—riding the bus, dancing in my room, or walking to church—my brain told me that I was just fine. When I got off the bus, I marched up and down Main Street with my heavy backpack and gawked at the iron gates and wraparound porches that made Chatmoss look like a condemned brothel. No one ever said they resented my uncles' gaudy, out-of-place apartments, but I suspected plenty of pearl-necked old ladies chirped about them over dinners on fine bone china.

On Wednesday nights, my mother and I went to church for a hot meal and youth group. "It's cheap," the Lady reminded me. Whatever was in walking distance of Chatmoss was fair game. We lived off church meals and scrambled eggs and toast and cans of tomato soup.

What was initially done in desperation became a boon. Like the Lady's "standing on our heads" method of marking minutes on a legal pad, I counted the hours until I was back at church, in an environment where people were required by sacred law to be nice to me.

The Lady couldn't afford to give me the middle school allowance my peers were getting. There weren't dance classes or tennis lessons or other extracurriculars for kids who had no after-school transportation or money to spend after school.

Instead, she gave me assignments from her self-help books: "Read this," she said, handing me Gail Sheehy's *Passages: Predictable Crises of Adult Life* and David Keirsey's *Please Understand Me: Character and Temperament Types.*

I was twelve.

When we got on our feet, the Lady took us out driving as a fun activity.

"Nothing makes you feel richer than a full tank of gas," King had always said.

"Daddy was always a little *manic,*" the Lady said, turning our white Oldsmobile Cutlass onto Highway 158. She'd bought the car when a great-great-uncle died childless and she and her siblings became heirs to his estate. We were headed to her father's grave on my mother's version of a midnight bike ride.

While my fellow middle schoolers spent their weekly allowance at the Pennrose Mall, the Lady drove me around on gallons of gas that cost less than a dollar. Like King's tours through his hometown of Dana, riding through Reidsville on what we called "cemetery cruising" was the Lady's form of cheap entertainment.

"I should have married John Young." She sighed. "But he was just *so* ugly. Joke's on me! He became a plastic surgeon!"

My mother's complicated relationship with men was a holdover from her southern youth. As the baby of five children, her primary coping skill was manipulation, mostly of men. Her adolescent pattern went as follows: Latch on to a powerful man, manipulate said man, find another man, turn the two men against each other until they catch on. Ditch them. Repeat.

"Mother took me to shop at Montaldo's with Daddy's money. It was her way of getting back at him for all the affairs. Have I told you how that Roberta *ruined* my wedding day by calling the church? She even threatened to kill me once."

Roberta had been my maternal grandfather's main side-lady.

Mom's daddy, Buck, had run an illegal slot machine business under the auspices of a family record company. He hoarded diamond jewelry and acreage and women while his staunch Baptist wife, my maternal grandmother, raised their brood. Within weeks of moving to Reidsville, I knew who was buried where and what escapades had sunk into the ground with them.

"See—over there. That's where Daddy built your aunt Ann's house," she said, pointing to a little brick ranch with modern glazing. "She used to hold me down and squeeze my blackheads, so I buried her favorite heart locket."

With the precision of a computer, my mother remembered wrongs done by her four siblings. But by all accounts, the Lady's upbringing had been comfortable. I would have taken some sibling torture if it meant steady shelter, food, and shopping trips.

Buck Trent's life had been productive, even if manic. He'd accrued a lot by the age of fifty-one: a steady business, a wife of three decades, five kids, acres, rental houses, and possibly some illegitimate children. Along with his assets, he'd gained diagnoses: bipolar and depression.

" 'Bye, baby. I love you'—those were the last words he said to me." The Lady recounted her father's death story at least once per week. She was nineteen and married to Lee's father. They hadn't yet moved to Ohio and lived thirty minutes from Reidsville at that time. Buck had insisted on leaving Reidsville's small-town hospital after a week's stay for his depression. He was set to receive electric shock treatment in a nearby city the day he committed suicide.

Just over thirty years later, the Lady and I pulled into the gravel cemetery drive off Highway 158. Buck rested near the front in a small plot with well-kept grass. Fresh flowers placed by Uncle Elton and Aunt Plum sat in a bronze vase on his marker, which was flush with the ground. I pressed the grass between my fingers as the Lady recalled details in a liturgy of remembrance. Like King with his midnight bike rides, the Lady had her own weekly rituals she was keen to initiate me into: Jailhouse nursing. Visiting my grandmother in her nursing home. Driving to the cemetery. Recounting the suicide.

Buck put his favorite revolver to his right temple on the Monday morning of the appointment while my grandma Evelyn was taking out the trash. His body slumped to the tile floor of the family bathroom and blocked the door. My grandfather had been raised by three paternal aunts when his own mother died young. Two of the aunties were politely termed "as crazy as bedbugs" by the rest of the family. Photos of his mother, who is buried in a secluded Trent family cemetery on the farm, depict her as beautiful and sweet. Buck told his five children often, "You don't know how fortunate you are."

The Lady was Buck's baby. She inherited the mental illness as well as a propensity for being what her siblings politely referred to as "spoiled rotten." Buck showered the Lady with cash for shopping sprees and trotted her out like a prized calf for local beauty pageants. When the Lady refused to attend kindergarten like all her siblings had, her father dismissed it as just fine. She clung to her mother's skirt until Buck got home each day, then followed him around like a lost puppy.

The Lady's relationship with her father was a lifelong source of contention. Her special treatment as the baby was an affront to the four older children in light of their hard-knocks upbringing. Uncle Charlie, the eldest of the five, was born the morning of the 1929 stock market crash and slept in a dresser drawer for most of his childhood. The second, Aunt Ann, suffered from a painful bone disease that required several childhood surgeries that confined her to a wheelchair during healing. She was tough as nails, refusing to accept any labels of disability. Uncle Elton upheld the stereotypes of a middle child like Uncle Leuge: independent, eager to establish his own path, head down, hardworking, and reliable. Uncle Elton had started driving a school bus as soon as he was legal and pulled cars out of ditches with a tractor for twenty dollars each. The last two children, my aunt Gail and the Lady, were born within two years of each other but five and seven years after Elton, so they seemed like an afterthought, although my Grandmother Evelyn had always insisted on five children. The littles hadn't had to experience the farm toil and empty bellies that the eldest siblings had endured.

The Lady wasn't even reading yet when she buried Aunt Ann's prized possession of a gold locket, and the beef between them never faded. Ann saw the Lady as idle. The Lady saw Ann as bossy. The Lady's siblings, for all the tension between them and her, doted on me like I was a newborn when we moved to Reidsville.

After her father's suicide, the Lady fell into an emotional collapse that culminated in postpartum depression after Lee was born. She saw a psychiatrist who prescribed a cocktail of uppers and downers that kept her as anxious as a polecat, but at least she could get out of bed. But on a day in May, Dude returned home from a rained-out softball game to find an unconscious wife who needed her stomach pumped. This was one of the Lady's many suicide attempts.

"I was so disappointed when I woke up," the Lady said, sitting in the driver's seat of the Olds with the door open as I lay in the grass by Buck's grave. That attempt was what had gotten her the three-month stay at Duke in the same inpatient unit where she'd worked.

"I couldn't wait to get on the inside," she said, jingling her keys like King used to do. "It was a real vacation."

"And I told Dude he'd better have that convertible waiting for me when I got out," she added. It was parked outside when she was released in August. "It was white. I wanted a blue one."

We spent hours at that cemetery. The Lady sat in the car and recalled stories of growing up on her father's farm: the 1950s prosperity, cows and gardens, pet monkeys and her deep affection for her father. There was even an isolated cemetery on the property, hidden behind hundred-year-old trees. When we visited it, the tombstones were barely legible, and a single plot of young grass marked where Buck had been exhumed not twenty years prior and transferred to this new, pristine spot. The Lady viewed this as equivalent to grave robbing. When my brother was little and she was home for a holiday, she drove the dirt road back to the old, private cemetery on the farm and pulled up to the rusted chain-link fence that kept our ancestors in their sleeping places. When she knelt to place daisies on Buck's tombstone, all that was left was fresh dirt.

"It's too hard to get back there," her siblings had told her, justifying the moving of his remains.

"No one tells the baby anything!" the Lady said to me, still angry at being left out.

But this new resting place off a busy highway was well manicured and still encircled by gravel. It worked out in the end: Her homeplace was ultimately bulldozed in favor of a strip mall. And this cemetery, where we spent many weekend hours, was where she taught me to drive. Like King taught me Hoosier lessons from the seat of a borrowed Schwinn, the Lady showed me her heritage from the front seat of the Olds.

By that first Halloween in her hometown, I was an expert in Trent family history and qualified to be a Reidsville tour guide. I knew my parents' background inside out—what happened where and to whom and how King and the Lady felt about it.

Then, that fall, King visited Chatmoss without an invitation.

"What do you think of *this,* Budge?" he said after I greeted him in the parking lot of our apartment complex. He opened a heavy door to a Corvette ZR1. The smooth white fiberglass with black trim was out of place in the dump of crumbling bricks and broken glass we called home. He'd emerged from the car in his signature overalls and Yankees cap.

When he hugged me, he smelled like the old trafficking days in the Ninth Street trailer: Old Spice, marijuana skunk, and Vaseline. I hadn't seen him since that Christmas. The scary psychosis I'd witnessed had evaporated from his hazel eyes.

"Rick," the Lady said, stern, holding open the Chatmoss storm door in her pink bathrobe.

"Judy," he replied.

They were civil enough toward each other, like two gentlemen tipping their hats in the public square. Her mood softened a little when he made mention of the cash he planned to spend on us. "I'm taking you both out," he said.

We were more desperate than we realized for his lavish and ostentatious gifts. Money was so tight at Chatmoss, the Lady and I jumped at the chance to do something besides going to the jail where she worked, church, or the cemetery. King drove us thirty minutes north to the closest mall, where he pulled out wads of Franklins from his overalls pockets, perplexing cashiers.

"Cognitive dissonance," he said, teeth clenched, handing me shopping bags. "These people don't know what to think!" He laughed.

"King Lewman, retired, state of Ohio, at your service," he'd said to a cashier at Wet Seal. The young teen studied this manic-eyed middle-aged man in the Yankees cap and holey shirt who handed him sweaty hundreds.

I could tell he was thinking, *Should we take his money or call the cops?*

The store clerk opted for the former, and I got a forest-green suede jacket and the *Nevermind* tape out of the deal. We were thirty minutes from school and church and Chatmoss, but I still kept a watchful eye out for any classmates.

With my new jacket on and "Smells like Teen Spirit" vibrating his Corvette speakers, I squished my middle-schooler frame against the back window as King sped us back to Reidsville with his Fuzzbuster like in the old drop days. The Lady sat in the passenger bucket seat.

We took the highway at ninety, and my parents whispered like close confidants.

For a moment, I wondered if they'd get back together.

When they were married, they fought about money and business. One would accuse the other of being lazy and crazy. But they were each prone to fits of listlessness and grandiosity. They were more nostalgic than they wanted to admit, inching toward each other with a recognition possible only for two people who have been ill, tortured, confined, outcast, and stuck in wild minds.

"Takes one to know one, huh?" I imagined King saying to the Lady over the thud of Nirvana.

"Tough times never last . . . but tough people do!" she'd respond and laugh.

They were like two peas in an eight-cylinder pod, rolling down the freeway, staking a claim to the one thing both of them cared about: whose daughter I would turn out to be.

NINE

Hoosier Summers

KING'S UNEXPECTED, LAVISH CORVETTE VISIT MADE ME long for home, whatever that meant.

I begged the Lady for a map of the United States, and she finally agreed to buy me one to hang on my Chatmoss bedroom wall. I sat on my top bunk and followed interstate lines with my fingertips, tracing the route from Reidsville to Dana.

Letters arrived and were sent. My pen-pal relationship with King strengthened to phone calls with him and G&GL, Aunt Marietta, Uncle Leuge, Lindah, and Doggy. These Indiana relationships were the well-kept secret of my North Carolina days. I lived a divided life, wondering how they spent their midwestern hours back home.

At church, I made friends with old and young people using strategies from the Lady's *How to Win Friends and Influence People*. By seventh grade, I was eagerly listening to octogenarians' stories and complaints, wishes fulfilled and dreams still unrealized. Like I had during midnight bike rides and cemetery cruising, I memorized the details of other people's lives. The meanness that climaxed with a sucker punch to George's face at Reidsville Middle School had evaporated. Since the day in Principal Ross's office when he'd called me a fireball, I'd tried very hard not to be a fireball.

"Pretty is as pretty does," the Lady said to me, fixing my slip before church.

"Your mother is *so* beautiful," the old folks at First Baptist Church would say after worship, recalling once again the Lady's early days in Reidsville. She beamed when they said it. It was as much a question as a comment, as in, *How had her daughter managed to arrive in her hometown with crooked teeth, a wide back, and thick glasses?* The Lady had been crowned "Miss Reidsville High 1956," a gaunt, pale beauty queen with chestnut hair and eyebrows and full lips, with porcelain collarbones protruding from the expensive gown Buck paid for with glee. Her regal portrait still hung in the old high school.

Besides the seniors I sat with at First Baptist Church Wednesday night suppers, there was no segment of the Reidsville population I tried harder with than boys. I was boy crazy.

Middle school and high school were marked by a steady stream of "talking" and "going together," the labels 1990s tweens and teens gave to dating. Boys were the arena in which Budgie was free to be confident, aggressive, and fierce, ready to conquer the male heart.

I accepted any and every invitation to "talk" or "go together." Most were stand-ins until something cuter came along. A few were crushes whose interest kept me floating for weeks. My daily journals were full of highs and lows, heartbreak, unrequited love, wish lists and to-dos so that God would land me (and let me keep) this boy or that one, as if they were kittens in need of good homes.

One of the best places to find boys was the First Baptist Church youth group. It was brimming over with enough testosterone to satisfy the fantasies of nineties evangelical Christian girls. Amid the angst of True Love Waits, we all signed up to save sex for marriage. But flirting was always on the table. In girls' Acteens missions small groups, we wrote "Dear Future Husband" letters that listed, in alphabetical order, the top-ten characteristics we all wanted in our Baptist spouses.

And if church was the land of silent lust, school was the Babylon of fantasies fulfilled.

"Boy crazy!" The small group of Reidsville Middle School girlfriends I'd managed to make cackled, rattling off the list of my crushes.

I was interested in any boy who showed me interest, and even those who didn't. In other words, I was the young woman who tried to replace her absent father's love and attention with external validation from the opposite sex.

But I was very careful about my reputation. "It's all we've got." The Lady was adamant.

Although I flirted and talked on the phone and held hands and even kissed boys, I upheld my True Love Waits teenage pledge.

Pubescent men were the source from which I derived all my energy. I didn't feel alive unless I was in the intrigue phase—plotting my next emotional seduction of a boy with sporty six-pack abs.

Books by Dale Carnegie and Tony Robbins, a book called *The Rules: Time-Tested Secrets for Capturing the Heart of Mr. Right,* and sexist evangelical Christian books on complementarian dating roles ultimately landed me the "Biggest Flirt" superlative and a place on homecoming court, the varsity cheerleading squad, and prom court.

"Boy crazy," Reidsville friends confirmed with each accolade.

My Chatmoss bunk beds were scribbled with boys' names written in thick Sharpie. I sat on my bed most nights, willing the phone to ring. Here, in the Lady's hometown, I stepped into my role as goody-goody youth group girl. I could no longer muster the tough edginess I'd shown at Reidsville Middle School before my bloody-knuckle visit to Principal Ross's office. It was too risky to act like that. Besides, it was bullying.

But instead of landing in the middle, I swung furiously to the other end of the spectrum away from meanness. I became saccharine and people-pleasing, starved for acceptance from others.

Amid my boy-obsessed years, King's Corvette visit catalyzed a reconnection with Vermillion County. Grandmother began to send letters to the Lady, working up the nerve to ask her if I could live with them in Dana for the summers. With no money to keep me occupied at middle school summer camps, the Lady said it was a splendid idea. The summer after sixth grade, I packed every suitcase and borrowed duffel bag and went to live with my grandparents for six weeks. My mother got a welcome break.

When I got off the plane, Grandmother squeezed me tight. She left her Chloé perfume and makeup on my T-shirt and said not to worry—this was going to be the best summer of my life. Though G&GL were alleged child-beaters, I'd never seen them even smack a fly. I only knew they were capable, grown adults. I was in awe of how they got out of bed and got dressed every day. They fixed me chocolate milk and instant oatmeal for breakfast and told me to take a load off and watch Regis and Kathie Lee. The only stipulation of living in Vermillion County for June and July was that I was not allowed to spend the night in whatever wreck of a trailer my father was squatting in. My grandparents and the Lady insisted on this rule.

The usual anxiety I felt over being away from my mother evaporated when I thought of spending time with G&GL, Lindah, Doggy, Aunt Marietta, Uncle Leuge, and King.

"Just have breakfast with me, Budge," King said when he called G&GL's one morning. We were listening to Regis tell a joke about his wife, Joy. "I want time with you and a nice meal," he persisted. I agreed.

My father picked me up in Dana for breakfast in Clinton. We took his two-door Cutlass back to town, where he wanted to show me his new-to-him trailer. "Nicest place you'll ever see. Middle of all the action!"

He was living in a rented 1960s single wide on Sycamore Street down from the NAPA Auto Parts store and across from Mills Restaurant.

By the time the green suede jacket he'd gotten me had turned shiny with everyday wear, the Ninth Street trailer had been condemned and hauled away. He'd used the same razor he'd trained me with to destroy everything. No square foot was left unsliced.

But I was now a budding teenager, self-conscious about my father's twitches and itches and dirty overalls and rabbinical beard. I was ashamed of the stolen cars and crucifixes and "Precious Jesus!" and "veeshuns." I didn't want to be seen with him in public in Clinton.

"You're King's daughter," my father said and held open

the glass door as a bell announced our arrival to the breakfast crowd. Hoosiers with flushed cheeks and leathery necks huddled together and hollered across the place in between drags on their cigarettes.

"King!" They waved us over and raised their coffee mugs to Michelle, who was waitressing.

Two men at the bar parted to make room for us to sit.

"Budgie's all grown up!" they said, slapping King on the back.

"She's the smartest Carolina girl you'll ever meet. Tough too. Like her old man." He threw his head back with a cackle and showed his vampire teeth.

Some were disciples I knew; others were a younger crowd my father had recruited in his current "Orthodox rabbi meets Indiana hillbilly-pirate" phase. King's white Corvette, like Big Red and other crucifix-decorated vehicles, had vanished. And along with it, my father's *Miami Vice* persona—one of the schizophrenic personalities he'd adopted when he began working with Carnival Captivations after moving back to Vermillion County from L.A. He burned his early-eighties aviators and pastel polos to ash after he snorted his last line of blow. Cocaine was expensive, he'd said and tossed his shirts into the trash barrel flames. He preferred cheaper speed anyway. Nothing like the "salt of the earth" life of a Jewish hillbilly, he insisted. Besides, the uppers kept him moving and the downers kept him from killing, he explained. This was King: You never knew what persona, outfit, vehicle, or mood you were going to get. But if you were a good buddy, you could count on his loyalty, no matter what he was wearing. If you weren't, you could count on getting your throat slit by his twitchy hand.

But at Mills Restaurant that morning, these were all good

buddies—worn men who were nicer to me than any southerners I'd met in North Carolina. I told King that. "Well, of course they are," he said. "You're the King's daughter."

After breakfast, he showed me his Sycamore Street trailer, which was such a dump that even the most rugged "college" graduates who'd shank their own brothers wouldn't set foot in it. It had rickety metal steps leading to an aluminum door that opened to a dark living room. Inside, King had covered the cabinets of his kitchen "office" with couch cushions. It was an attempt to trap the rodents in and keep government bugs out. "They can't hear a thing," he said. The bedrooms were bare, and the bathroom was covered in black mold. Beside the TV, a wooden altar inscribed with "Shalom" held his King James Bible.

"This is the ole homeplace," he told me, arms out like he was showing me my inheritance. His kiddie-ride trafficking money was gone; Viper had dissolved the business without much fuss and disappeared. I never knew if it was King who stepped away or if Viper fired him.

Cuffs—not "college"—was the deterrent Vermillion County sheriffs now used when King exhausted their patience. He'd been arrested a few times outside his hovel for false informing and disturbing the peace. "No big deal," he said.

"You're gonna help me spruce up the joint," he said and showed me cans of paint he'd lifted.

It was like spraying air freshener on the Dana shit ditch.

By sixth grade I'd learned that my parents, whether they were in Indiana or North Carolina, were into quick fixes: a gallon of paint here, fancy *JTL Enterprises* stationery there. What harm was a burned bridge, a cutoff, or a bankruptcy? None, according to them.

I sighed and picked up a paintbrush King had fished out of the NAPA dumpster.

"Thou shall not trim the corners of thy beard," King told his mother when he dropped me off that night back in Dana. Nothing had changed between them since the night we slurped brown cows after the midnight bike ride that ended with King's feigned "leever" attack. I hadn't missed a thing, except that King now had full blown hepatitis C.

"Oh, for land's sake, Rick," she said. "You need to cut that dreadful beard." They were yelling in the kitchen as we sat down to a Chef Boyardee supper Grandmother had made to welcome me home. My father's beard was still covered in that morning's eggs, and his mother was aghast.

"Leviticus 19:27!" he hissed. "Read your Bible, *Dorothy*. You ungodly woman!"

"You'd look so much better if you didn't go around looking like a hillbilly!" she said in her low, gruff tone.

I half expected them to come to blows over the spaghetti, but King was hungry, so he sat down to eat. Lindah, Doggy, Aunt Marietta, and Uncle Leuge were silent; the only sound we all heard was King's smacking lips. He always chewed with his mouth open.

"Good supper, Dorothy," he said, quieted by a full belly. King got up after he finished his plate in just under five minutes. He walked out the door and to his car for tokes off his freshly rolled joint.

I finished my meal slowly, then checked on him outside.

He was leaning against the Cutlass when I walked up. "Your grandmother is a pharisee! You remember that," he said.

I nodded. It was no use arguing.

"And your no-good grandfather denied our Jewish roots!

They are both going to hell," he added. "That son of a bitch changed our name." King was convinced that our Lewman surname was actually Jewman.

"German cocksucker." King spit into his bandana. An obsession with our family's Jewishness had replaced the religion of Dr. Schuller and the devotion to kiddie-ride drug trafficking.

In the early 1990s, King began insisting we were all Jewish. Neither of my grandparents agreed with this narrative. He grew his curly hair long beneath his Platchige hat until it looked like *payot*. When he wore a stolen black suit and spouted Leviticus 19:27 with his own Mishnah, ironically in King James English, his performance was convincing.

But all Grandmother wanted to know was why he kept a statue of Mother Mary in his front yard and glued a crucifix to the dashboard of every vehicle he ever drove.

"Because they were *Jewish*!" he rebutted.

Grandmother made up my sofa bed in the "pink room" of the apartment where I'd live with them for the next six weeks. The brand-new mauve carpet and floral-bloom prints mirrored her personality: feminine, jovial, optimistic. In contrast to my own southern mother, King's mother was the kind of Savannah-born-and-bred woman who took care of body, mind, and environment—and urged you to do the same. Grandmother stood on her own two feet: perky and social but not naïve. As an army nurse, she'd seen men blown to pieces. Even though she preferred the rosier side of life, she was no fool. That comforted me.

In her own bedroom, Grandmother kept the vanity where she dabbed on thick makeup and adjusted her blond wigs. She blotted her smooth skin with a foundation-soaked sponge, then lined her eyes and filled in her eyebrows with a

blue pencil. Her cerulean brows made her look like a surprised Joan Crawford, but she didn't balk. She never cared
what grandmothers *should* look like. Grandmother was a
natural beauty who loved artificial beauty. She wore tacky
hats superglued with fake dahlias, red cowgirl shirts, and mis-
matched bangles that clanged while she told stories about
growing up in Savannah. Her clip-on rhinestones made her
lobes hang down, and her hands were heavy with gold and
diamonds mixed with quarter rings she bought at flea mar-
kets. You knew which was which by the thick green bands the
cheap stuff left behind on her fingers.

"Grandmother looks *lovely*," she said when she was satisfied with her day's look.

"Grandmother looks *lovely*," Lindah, Doggy, and I repeated after her.

The days after I arrived in Vermillion County that summer were slow enough to savor, and I quickly fell into Grandmother's routine. She took me to her Clinton aerobics classes,
and Grandfather pulled his Lumina van out of the garage so
my cousins and I could dance on the linoleum tiles that kept
his oil off the concrete. G&GL encouraged me to take bike
rides and move and be a kid.

Grandmother signed Lindah, Doggy, and me up for jitterbug lessons in the Dana firehouse, where a blond smoker
we called "Judy Bags" taught us the wartime steps to the
sound of the Glenn Miller Orchestra. Back at G&GL's apartment, we practiced on Grandfather's garage linoleum to the
smell of gasoline, wearing out any cassette tape with thirty-
two-count tracks. We sweated until supper, when Grandmother had every living member of her family sit at the table
and again eat a slow dinner of Chef Boyardee candy spaghetti
and white bread.

That first summer home, I was steeped in the lives of two World War II veterans keen on teaching us what life in the 1940s had been like. Over porridge, Grandmother recalled USO shows and the Andrews Sisters. When she talked about journalist Ernie Pyle being born in Dana, her eyes shimmered.

"Time for the museum tour!" she'd say before clearing breakfast dishes and ushering me out of the house and down the alley with her to learn my namesake's history.

Ernie was born in Dana in 1900 and died in action in Japan just five months before the war ended. The 1851 clapboard house where he was born and raised is a state historic site and on the National Register of Historic Places. The house and museum with Quonset huts are full of his stories and artifacts.

At the end of our tour, my cousins and I would slip out the back, past the Quonset huts, and down the alley, back to G&GL's apartment to eat Oreos and drink Cokes until Grandmother noticed we were missing.

Prior to his combat death, Ernie Pyle gave the American public their first colloquial, personal real look at war and its effects on the everyday soldier. His legacy gave life to the town. Dana still holds an annual end-of-summer festival in Ernie's honor. The volunteer fire department blocks off the roads for the three-day celebration of Ernie Pyle, the troops, and 1940s nostalgia. When Lindah, Doggy, and I were young, Main Street was lined with fair-food trucks, while alleys and parking lots overflowed with flea market dealers selling candy cigarettes for twenty-five cents. The festival's programs are printed in purple "Dana Aggie" ink, the same hue as the defunct Dana High School mascot. The booklet was packed with festivities that signaled an end to July's hot monotony.

That summer, I finally got to join in the celebration.

Twenty paces from the plastic lawn chairs set up all along Main Street, we popped in and out of G&GL's apartment, running through carny tents and elephant ear stands. King drove up from Clinton. Crowds of a thousand people smooshed into a town just over a quarter of a square mile big, eager to honor Ernie, parading their tractors and corn combines down Main Street. Kids gathered in the center of the street on the spray-painted cakewalk circles and performed their talent-show routines. My Lewman family introduced me to the tradition of gorging on landlocked seafood at the Jonah Fish Fry and slurping noodle dinners. Grandmother emptied her closet of dresses and streamers, decorating her three granddaughters for bike contests. She coached us from the sidelines as we danced off our fried food in jitterbug contests while King cupped his hands to his mouth and hollered at us to beat out all the "no-good pirates" dancing beside us. We spent the dollars Grandfather gave us tossing rings onto longneck bottles in rigged carnival games.

Most evenings during those Indiana summers, Lindah, Doggy, and I asked to be excused from Grandmother's supper table to resume King's midnight bike ride rituals. My father picked up right where he'd left off, entertaining us with gang stories and training us in bicycle martial arts.

"Dog Town!" he yelled when we pedaled to the south side of Dana by the railroad tracks. It was known for its rotting buildings with smashed windows, and its ominous lack of human presence suggested that mean abandoned canines lived there, hunting for scraps of whatever trash was left behind by trains or littering drivers. We'd never seen an actual dog in Dog Town, but King insisted we learn to defend ourselves against an attack.

Those midnight bike rides, just like when I was younger,

were exposure therapy—King's preferred psychological and tactical training. He guided us three nervous girls on bikes in the pitch black. We were taught to lift our strongest foot off the pedal, balance the bike, and kick invisible rabid animals.

"Kick, girls, kick! Kill or be killed!" King shouted.

The rule of combat I'd learned as a small child applied now too: Be ready to explode. Dog Town lessons were my father's time to shine. In the dark night of that sleepy town, I wasn't as ashamed of him. But the daylight reminded me of who he really was: scruffy, paranoid, and sick.

Every June and July starting that first summer when I was twelve, King taught me a new skill like painting a nasty trailer, Jewish law, or fighting off Cujos in Dog Town. The summer I turned fourteen, King taught me to drive, his way. While the Lady's doldrum cemetery driving lessons implored me to practice among the dead, my father's method matched his parenting: alive, reckless, and at full tilt.

"Now this is important, Budge." He paused and pressed his greasy fingers to the crucifix on his dash. "Someone's coming at you? You hit the gas. You knock that cocksucker right out of the way!"

The night we hit the deer rushed back, and the smell of burnt fur filled my nose.

My parents lived by this rule: Be aggressive, forceful, explosive. Although they interpreted this ideology in different ways, the gift of their mental illness was complete unawareness—they had no self-consciousness about destruction, just like the Lady proved when she ran Viper's truck off the snowy Buffalo road, nearly making me an orphan.

By the end of that summer, I was driving too fast on blacktops back and forth to the Clinton Walmart and Terre Haute with King as my passenger. He didn't smoke joints in front of me in those days, probably for fear I'd rat him out to G&GL and our summer visits would cease. It was for the best. By my Reidsville Middle and High School days, I'd become an anti-drug evangelical Christian, reading from my own worn King James Bible every night before bed.

But breaking the law never fazed me. When King insisted I drive on highways at age fourteen, I didn't flinch. When the Lady wanted me to practice parking in a cemetery, I was enthusiastic. But my crimes always grabbed me by the collar and made me pay in a way my parents never experienced.

One day at Buck's cemetery, I backed the Lady's white Olds into a meemaw's granite memorial bench. Then I put the car in drive and sped away like King would have advised. But the Lady, who'd broken many statutes in her five decades, got a conscience and made me turn back. I spent the next semester of Saturdays bagging groceries at Winn-Dixie to pay for that slab of engraved rock.

The busted bench was evidence of their paradoxical parenting: a push-pull of breaking rules when it suited them and following them when it didn't. The Lady insisted that I pay for the granite only because we were in her small hometown. She feared for her reputation. King's advice to commit any crime *and* leave any crime scene—even in Vermillion County—was indicative that he didn't give a flip about reputations.

King and the Lady both had their methods of manipulation.

For the Lady, it was subtle and emotional.

For King, it was direct and skillful. How could he play you while you were playing? As a certified recreational therapist, King knew every game in the book and how, through activities and parties and fun, to get you to talk and give him whatever he wanted.

When King came to Dana for midnight bike rides those summers I was home, we'd spend a few hours before dark on Main Street at Dana's only video rental store, which tripled as a pool hall and hardware store. King put spare change in the jukebox and played "Hey Jude" on repeat, channeling Paul Newman and Tom Cruise in *The Color of Money*.

"Luck itself is an art," he'd remind me.

"Eight ball, corner pocket," I said, tapping my stick against the edge of the table like he'd taught me.

"Aim low," he said. "Watch them brakes."

"There you go, Budge." He beamed when the pool ball sank into the pocket. "Now, you never let these boys know your old man taught you how to play. You suck them in first. Make them lay down their money. Then you hand them their asses." He tapped me on the shoulder with a cue. "You got it?"

My father's boyhood repeated itself when I first realized that some people in Vermillion County liked to make fun of Dana. A big constituency of Clintonians called us scum, but my family never saw themselves that way. Neither did I.

Even so, my teenage summers home were marked by plastic above-ground pools, a symbol of poor white America. While rich people in Clinton had limestone houses and poured concrete pools dug with backhoes, anyone with two pennies to rub together in Dana found themselves swimming in a giant Tupperware container from Walmart. Lindah, Doggy, and I flipped our hair into George Washington wigs in Aunt Marietta and Uncle Leuge's above-ground pool behind the Lewman Museum until dark. Aunt Marietta caught our shiny rear ends in the moonlight when she looked out her kitchen window after scrubbing the dinner dishes.

The girls and I fell into a summer routine as fun as any

days I'd ever lived. My cousins were my best friends—sisters to me, really—and our Junes and Julys were marked by belting out songs coming from the boom box Leuge kept for us by his pool.

Before Lindah got her license, our fathers drove us all across the Wabash River into Montezuma after supper at Grandmother's. While King and Leuge caught up on NBA playoff buzz and Vermillion County gossip in the front seat, we sang "The Time of My Life" from the *Dirty Dancing* soundtrack. We rode in the back like we were starring in MTV music videos, bathing in the lush summer landscape of our hometown.

We were too punch-drunk in love with this land to even notice the stench of the pig farm or the crop fertilizer runoff allegedly poisoning its residents. Our youth was light and innocent; I never even told the girls about my lookout training or the switchblade in King's pocket or the sawed-out trapdoor under his kitchen recliner or his suicidal threat that Christmas. I just wanted to be normal: the kind of girl who didn't have mentally ill parents or know about dead great-grandfathers floating in the Wabash River or concrete buckets lowered into black water. I wanted to pretend that I was too young to know—or understand—and that I'd been raised with more luck than I deserved.

"You can get away with murder in Vermillion County, girls," Leuge said yet again, interrupting our rendition of Otis Redding's "Love Man."

King swiped his nose with his crimson handkerchief and nodded toward the green-and-white sign that read, "Now entering Parke County."

"Not here, girls," my father added.

Squeezed into the back seat, the trio of us girls were reminded that villains came in every age and motivation, not just with Vincent Price–esque salt-and-pepper widow's peaks and waxed mustaches.

"It's a tough world out there, girls. Dog-eat-dog, and the one with the sharpest teeth wins," Leuge told us. "When you leave Vermillion County, ninety percent of the people you'll meet in this world are idiots." The remaining ten percent included the members of our family.

Illinois was always the mathematical exception and rose easily to 100 percent idiot according to our fathers. When Lindah got her license, she drove us across the state line for floats at the Frostop where she waitressed during the summer.

"Be on the lookout at all times," Leuge coached her.

But the adults trusted her to cart me and Doggy around like two little dolls she found in the Barbie aisle at Toys "R" Us. During those summers, we took country roads at ninety like King, kicking up dust as we headed west to the Illinois Subway for lunch and east to the Ritz Theater in Parke County for choreography practice directed by her. We were always back in Dana for our own jitterbug dance lessons.

For the first time, I felt taken care of.

After my fourteenth birthday, I noticed that Indiana boys were just as handsome as the North Carolina youth group crop. The world—or regions of America—opened: I could date southern *and* midwestern men. When one harvest disappointed, the other came through. Having two sets of crops in rotation was good for the soil, I rationalized.

The truth was that having Indiana loves kept me tied to my heritage. King, more than anyone, was thrilled. The way he saw it, I was back to putting roots down in Vermillion County.

Jonathan was one of those loves. He was a year older

than me, tall and skinny with a coffee-colored buzz cut and blue eyes. He was demure, not really a troublemaker but running with them, a smart way of staying in the crowd without getting the Dana town cop on your tail. He lived with his mom one street over from Aunt Marietta and Uncle Leuge's and drove a two-door beater that was more iridescent than white, like someone had accidentally brushed it with speed-limit-sign paint. We flirted all summer and kept talking when I returned to Reidsville. He was a secret source of confidence, hidden in long-distance calls and love letters. Jonathan was a prized souvenir, like the T-shirt a grandma mails her grandkid that reads, "Somebody in Indiana Loves Me." Landing fly-over boys was so easy with a budding southern accent. Besides, they were less uptight and snobby than the Reidsville High School jocks I flirted with in the halls. And if Hoosier boys rejected me, their apathy was hundreds of miles away.

My preoccupation with Jonathan fizzled by Halloween, replaced by church boys with letter jackets and thick hair. But the danger with North Carolina guys was their proximity. They were like a hot stove ready to burn me when I hovered too close.

My obsession with boys continued each Indiana summer. I rotated through members of the modern Dana gang, descendants of our fathers' generation. Some drove Trans Ams or rode bicycles; others smoked or drank or played pool. If they were keen on trouble, I was keen on them.

Then I met Tommy. My hair was highlighted blond, and my eyebrows were waxed too thin—two trends that remain in vogue in Vermillion County. Tommy rocked platinum highlights and a tennis player's build: powerful legs, chiseled core, and lean arms. His tan skin complemented his light green eyes, and he spoke at a pace that told you he was really thinking hard about the world. He told me he'd never seen a southern belle as cute as me, not even in the movies. I slurped my pop and drew my shoulders back in my busty tank top. The first night we talked, we devoured each other like we were in a no-hands pie-eating contest, our feet dangling in an above-ground pool. He etched himself on my teenage heart with handwritten love letters on college-ruled paper.

But on King's watch, Tommy had to be initiated into our Lewman family rituals. If he and I were going to date for years or, hell, even get married, Tommy would have to endure my father's scrutiny during a half-hour drive to Terre Haute.

"I'll sit back here," I told Tommy, keeping a baby pool's depth of space between us in the back seat, which made King mad.

"You get up front with me, young lady," King said and snapped his fingers like he was calling a dog, just as he had when I was a preschooler. I rode shotgun.

As we took country road "shortcuts" at ninety, King got serious about Tommy getting serious. Though my boyfriend found my father's overalls, Vaseline-smeared face, and Yankees hat charming, he didn't know there was a fifty-fifty chance King was going to shank him. *I've dumped lighter loads,* King was thinking.

King believed victory in a fight hinged on proximity. You couldn't defeat your opponent unless you kept him close and surprised him. And nothing shocks even Vermillion County boys (or anyone) who believe themselves invulnerable more than looking them square in the eye and telling them you'll kill them.

"Any coward can pull a trigger," King said, changing the subject to guns, unprompted.

"Sir?" Tommy said.

"You like guns, kid?" King asked.

"No, sir," Tommy said.

"Knives?" King asked.

"Ugh, no, sir," Tommy said.

King grunted, disappointed that he'd put an unworthy opponent in his back seat.

"You smoke, kid?" King asked as his Cutlass launched over a hill.

"No, sir," Tommy said. He played tennis and golf and worked at the Raccoon Lake boat dock until his bronzed abs were etched into a six-pack.

If nothing else, my father was a salesman. He probably had a lip baggie and rolling papers waiting in the glove box.

"What is your course of study, young man?" King asked through clenched teeth, just like he did when saying, "We're on a tight schedule"—impersonating rich people on TV who knew the difference between a Triple Crown and Crown Royal.

"Haven't given it much thought yet," Tommy said.

That was the wrong answer.

King valued education as much as he valued his inventory.

The three of us bumped down the back roads of Vermillion County until I was carsick. We were four hours into a thirty-minute drive, and I was certain King was just looking for a wet cornfield to bury Tommy in when we finally pulled into the MCL cafeteria at Honey Creek Mall. I breathed out relief.

Over lunch, King ate in the disgusting way that infuriated Grandmother. Mouth open, showing his vampire teeth and the marks they left on his lips, shoveling food to the back of his throat like he was digging a grave. King finished his Salisbury steak in three minutes. Tommy and I ate quietly and slowly while King entertained us with his own educational ninja course at Indiana State University, where he'd driven the hearse and been arrested for mooning onlookers on Wabash Avenue.

In those cult leader years at ISU, it was nothing for him to impersonate professors and officers to keep his good buddies and disciples enrolled in school.

"Cognitive dissonance," King explained.

"Uh-huh." We both nodded, unsure what it meant.

He finished with a story about a 1948 Chevy he bought from Uncle Leuge for forty dollars in the mid-sixties. The car came with a free trunkload of military MREs and the rats who nibbled on them. King dumped the car in Times Square and hitchhiked to Georgia. The Rat-Trap had been a replacement for the hearse, which he sold to an unwitting hippy named Ducky, a New Yorker. We hadn't asked about either.

"Let's get going," King finally said and waited for Tommy to pick up the cafeteria bill. My teenage boyfriend removed the Velcro wallet from his pocket and paid for all of our lunches. King tapped his overalls and laughed. He had a band of cash duct-taped to his chest.

"Bless, bless," King said, pressing the crucifix as he slid into the Cutlass, cherry air fresheners swinging from the rearview. One corner of the car ceiling drooped; he snapped his blade out of his pocket, cut the lining off, and threw it on the ground. "Precious Jesus!" King shouted, like he was blessing his own littering.

Tommy marveled at my father's willingness to tear up his own car and bestow his "rabbinic" anointing on trash and people in equal measure.

"I have a *veeshun* for you," King said to us, backing the

Cutlass out of the mall parking space. "You shall be blessed with three sons from the descendants of Abraham." He spit into his bandana and recalled the prophecy from my early drug-drop days. "You shall name them James, Joshua, and Joseph," he forecasted, listing the three middle names he claimed were on his own birth certificate. James was the great-grandfather whom Gramps had pushed off a homemade raft into the Wabash.

King drove us past his favorite county bar by way of the back roads.

"Tickle top!" he'd shout when the Cutlass sped down a gravel hill so fast that our lunches lurched up into our throats.

"Butt boy," King said when we got back to G&GL's and as Tommy drove away in the Chevy he'd parked when the sun was still high in the sky. We leaned against King's dirty Olds, silent.

I knew Tommy wasn't the one, but I wasn't ready to admit it.

I left Indiana the next week. August pulled me back to a new North Carolina school year and the boredom that was alleviated only by a series of new crushes. Boys were my drugs. My high school journal pages were packed with uppers of flirtation and downers of rejection. Despite Tommy's offering of a consistent, loving relationship, my craving for attention was as relentless as an addict's insistence on "just this one hit."

But I dated Tommy seriously for years after that; he kept me tethered to a place I longed for but wasn't allowed to call home.

| TEN |

Salem Spirits and Blue Devils

S UMMERS IN VERMILLION COUNTY HAD REKINDLED MY connection with the Lewman family, which hurt my relationship with the Lady. Navigating time with my parents was a losing game of Whac-A-Mole. If I met the deficit with one, the other would pop up. It was as much about hatred for each other as it was about love for me or parental self-esteem.

And the Lady's self-esteem was basement low. But not in the way sad teenagers like me thought about how nobody liked them or how ugly they were. Hers was the kind of confidence puzzle that keeps you moving pieces around for days. It manifested as meanness, then obnoxious self-importance that covered her insecurity. The only time she softened was if I went to her with a problem—a mental-health symptom. That buoyed her spirits like a sugar rush.

My long-term relationship with Tommy and the increased frequency of my Indiana visits only agitated the Lady. To make matters worse, I even asked to spend a high school Christmas with G&GL, and Tommy flew me home for his prom. Instead of feeling joy that I'd found love and reconnected with my roots, my mother was testy.

These milestones were troubling for her. What began as much-needed Indiana summer childcare morphed into a cause for resentment. She felt forgotten. The year-round single-parent martyrdom she'd endured in raising me had gone unnoticed. After so many transactions, the balance in her account of love was running low. In her eyes, she'd sacrificed everything to raise me: a career, money, dating—happiness. Years of debt with Dr. Gloria and a shit job on her feet nursing in a smelly health department wasn't how she'd imagined her life would turn out. Miss Reidsville High was home—broke, defeated, with only a budding adolescent daughter to show for it. I was her prize—an emotional support animal trained to anticipate and meet her every need. She had groomed me as her caregiver, and I was slipping from her grip.

The spring I turned eighteen, she began suggesting a name change.

Lewman was hard to spell; most folks wanted to write it as "Lumen" or the traditionally Jewish "Lehmann."

"It's L-E-W," I'd say. "*Lew* like *Mountain Dew.*"

After the divorce, the Lady had returned to her maiden name. Trent had name recognition in Chapel Hill and Reidsville. There were rich Trents tied to Duke University; there were rich Trents tied to our sleepy tobacco town. My North Carolina aunts, uncles, and cousins were all Trents—wealthy, admired, respected, upper class.

My surname made me feel like an outsider; it didn't connect me with my mother, and there were no Lewmans in Reidsville to show that these were, in fact, my family. Names, King and the Lady had taught me, told people who you were. According to my father, street names warned enemies and comforted good buddies. Mom said surnames indicated class. I just wanted to belong.

The Lady made an appointment with her lawyer as soon as I could legally declare myself a Trent. Once I graduated from high school, eighteen years of "Lewman" was expunged from my legal identity as if by a kid with a pink eraser. Through me, my mother rid herself of all remnants of her Indiana life. It was the beginning of a formal, certified separation from my heritage, my home, my father, and my family.

But changing my name was just the start. Refining my personhood was next. "You know Mother never let *me* go to Saint Mary's," the Lady said, bringing a tray of soft scrambled eggs to my bunk bed. I stared at all the boys' names I'd inscribed in Sharpie. In Mom's 1950s heyday, Saint Mary's was an Episcopal college-prep girls' high school for North Carolina debutantes.

"Wonderful, wonderful! Turn off the bubble machine!" the Lady had shouted the evening before when my Salem College acceptance letter and financial-aid packet arrived at Chatmoss. Salem was the early 2000s collegiate equivalent to Saint Mary's: a four-year charm school for southern ladies whose family legacy and pockets were as deep as the school's Moravian roots.

But I was listless.

"You know it's a *finishing* school." She chewed a bite of my eggs. "My work here is done, so they'll take care of the rest." She smiled and brushed her hands like she'd completed her eighteen-year-long parental to-do list.

"My life would have turned out *so differently* if Mother had allowed me to go to Saint Mary's."

It was typical of her to rewrite her life in what-ifs that hinged on other people instead of her own choices.

And by "differently," she meant a kept woman. It wasn't her dream to be a bankrupt single mother saddled with a delinquent Vermillion County daughter raised as King's Carnival Captivations lookout. The Lady, after all, saw herself the way Buck had seen her: a cherished prize who needn't dirty her hands with work or the likes of poor folk.

"I should have married John Young," she said, repeating her mantra from the Reidsville cemetery tours of my middle school years. I could predict verbatim her next statement: "But he was just *so* ugly," she reminded me.

"Joke's on me! He became a plastic surgeon!" I said in unison with her.

Now she was "kept" by me and Lee and her brothers, on whom she relied for moral and financial support.

After I graduated from high school, the Lady let me know that she would "retire" from her health department nursing job. It was a job she'd had for seven years, she said, the longest she'd ever held one position. "And I did it all for you," she added. It was a page out of King's book to let go of a good job, taking an "early retirement" she would never admit mirrored his own laziness when quitting his recreational therapy job in Ohio. The Lady had fallen out with her supervisor but thankfully made it to age sixty. She was able to collect Dude's social security check under a "widow's benefit," despite their contentious divorce.

She was barely existing on $1,200 a month, so Salem's offer looked good to a Pell Grant adolescent living below the poverty line in her uncles' apartments.

I sighed and took a bite of eggs. Salem would be the best education student loans could buy.

"Oh well. You're all I need," the Lady said and snapped from her "kept" daydream. "And you know what would taste so good right now?" she added.

"A fresh pot of coffee," I said.

"You know me so well! Now, get up and act like you're somebody!" the Lady said. "My Salem girl!"

I pushed aside my comforter like it was made of lead and shuffled downstairs to make her coffee.

My Reidsville High School tenure had been packed to the brim with academics and extracurriculars I'd hoped would get me into Duke. It was all I wanted. A prestigious International Baccalaureate program, offices in student government and leadership, internships, cheerleading, volunteering, a job—the hours of homework and labor and stretching now felt pointless. Dr. Yancy's elementary school testing had shown that I had an impressive IQ but lacked tenacity. That data explained why I'd scored barely over 1100 on the SAT. Duke undergrads scored 1600 without breaking a sweat.

Though my mother had cross-stitched her Duke daydreams of *Eruditio et Religio* for me in the Ninth Street trailer, I hadn't been accepted as an undergrad. The Lady's college "veeshun" of me attending Duke would have to wait.

But she wasn't let down, like I thought she'd be. The Lady had visited Old Salem during a break at a nursing conference. She was enamored with its early American charm, Moravian meekness, and devotion to single-sex education that would ward off my boy craziness. The way she told it, she'd experienced a miracle as real as my L.A. birth narrative: On the Salem Square, as she nibbled Moravian cookies and admired the pristine grounds, warm light poured out from a Dutch cottage door. It was the Salem College admissions office. In her eyes, Salem was now a perfectly good runner-up. I packed my bags.

The Salem College campus is nestled against Old Salem, a historic site that hosts far too many elementary school field trips to see "the pilgrims." Moravians balk at such historical inaccuracy. But they are far too long-suffering to chastise the delinquent children who call them that and who care more about buying miniature firecracker poppers in the gift shop than about learning the art of making ginger cookies as thin as airmail stationery. Visitors gorge themselves on sugar cakes from the bakery just off the Salem Square.

When I enrolled, the Old Salem grass was so pristine, I was convinced the landscapers trimmed it with nail clippers. A single horse lived in a twenty-by-twenty shed there, with no evident function save for historical ambience.

The two worlds of well-manicured eighteenth-century American cosplay and college students slammed together in the Square, where the administrators objected to bikini-clad Salem students pre-tanning for spring break trips to Myrtle Beach. On formal nights, we drove both the horse and the deans crazy by gathering on the grass to wait for "drunk buses," shuttles that ferried us to and from the bars and dance clubs. Sister Elisabeth Oesterlein, the first Salem College teacher, who dedicated her life to women's education, must have rolled over in her flat Moravian grave when Mardi Gras arrived and drunk women in purple, green, and yellow sequins pulled down their thongs to pee in the Square. We were in a constant battle with the higher-ups: rebels ruining the tourist and tuition trap of the money-minded adults.

The August air hung heavy as the Lady and I heaved my suitcases up to my third-floor single in Salem College's Gramley freshman dorm. I'd brought too much. Trinkets and high school photos and holy relics of dried flowers and rocks—anything that could help me feel loved and valued.

Gramley was the Siberia of Salem dorms since it was the farthest building from the Square. Everything about it screamed "stepchild," from the neglected sidewalks with heaving bricks that tripped you into a face-first fall to our disgruntled dorm mom we called "Mean Marge."

Gramley freshwomen soon found out that there were two dorms assigned to first-year students: our dump and Babcock, the country-club residence hall. After one week of comparing notes, our gaggle of eighteen-year-old geographical rejects deduced how we'd gotten stuck with the bad bricks and Mean Marge: Babcock was for the girls with cash; Gramley was for the working class. During dorm meetings in our moldy basement, we dramatized stories of administrators dividing Salem's class of 2003 into two stacks according to the thickness of our financial-aid packages. Mine was an encyclopedia of loans, grants, work study, and leadership scholarships. I'd even borrowed the extra six hundred dollars for my single room.

"It'll keep out the riffraff," the Lady had said, approving.

An Indiana summer is intolerable without an above-ground pool, but nothing is more miserable than a North Carolina summer without air-conditioning. We wiped sweat from every body part and posed for move-in photos with strained smiles and cheeks beet red from the heat.

Those first nights at Gramley, we made handfuls of friends by force, attending hall and dorm meetings to protest about the humidity and living in the reject dorm. At nine, I closed my single door and forced open the paint-peeling window that overlooked Salem's only student parking lot. The

Lady never allowed open doors and cracked windows to let in fresh air at home. "I'm allergic," she'd insist. But it wasn't the view or the breeze that charmed me; it was the freedom.

But by eleven, I was lonely, so I'd slide an illegal two-burner hot plate out from underneath my bed to boil myself generic box mac 'n' cheese with milk and butter, despite having a fully loaded Refectory meal plan. I ate my second dinner most nights at the window.

Salem sisters called our meal hall "The Rat," which displeased purse-lipped deans. The food was as decent as you can get cooking for the masses. I wasn't picky. The Lady's Chatmoss menu was composed of canned tomato soup and buttered saltines browned in a toaster oven. If she was feeling spry, she'd make scrambled eggs. So I ate my fill, stuffing my mouth with "free" food that made me feel less lonely.

With no AC, the Gramley window stayed propped open until Halloween. I watched girls come and go from the parking lot "Pit." We were informed that security guards were hired to escort Salem women from their parked cars to their dorms' doors after dark. Night after night, I watched as girls huffed up the hill, belting out curse words at the Salem public safety officer who insisted that only one woman could ride on the golf cart at a time, forcing the other girl to wait or walk in the dark.

"Doesn't that defeat the purpose?" students would argue.

"Rules is rules." The officer would shrug and ride off with one lucky passenger.

"Rent-a-cops!" the walker would shout as they rode away, her middle finger in the air.

That first semester, I clung to the only other Reidsville girl in my Salem freshman class. Since I had no roommate, her friends became my friends. We bonded over our annoyance with Mean Marge and the cafeteria food. But I secretly loved Gramley and never-ending food. It was a reprieve from trailers and Chatmoss and hunger and parents whose minds I fretted over. At college, I was responsible only for myself.

I was still dating Tommy, who was a year behind me in school. The spring of my freshman year at Salem, he bought me a plane ticket to fly home to Indiana to attend his senior prom.

He picked me up in Indianapolis, and his two-door Chevy barreled down Highway 36 in the late-spring greens. The Midwest was barely breaking through its gray winter. This was why Grandmother never planted her geraniums until Mother's Day.

The day of prom, Lindah and Doggy made me up in the bedrooms where they'd spent hours getting fixed up for the South Vermillion High School dances. We played our summer mixtapes and daydreamed about my moving back and marrying the Indiana boy who was crazy about me.

Our fantasies were interrupted by King's diesel truck jerking into Leuge's front yard. He said he'd "taken it off the hands" of a friend who needed quick cash. My father emerged from the cab in a beige polo with a curled-up collar. He was beaming.

G&GL, Aunt Marietta, Doggy, and Lindah stood in the tender May grass with flashing cameras. The Lady didn't make a fuss over photos before the Reidsville proms I'd attended—film for our 1980s Polaroid was hard to come by and expensive. My school-bus-yellow disposables were embarrassing, so I relied on friends' parents to pose and snap us.

But here, in the sunset of a windy Indiana spring, it was

the Lewmans who were doting and smiling and hugging and posing and snapping and laughing and crying. It was the first life-stage rite of passage they'd shared with me since my sixth birthday.

Tommy, handsome in his white tux, slid a corsage onto my wrist and hugged my red-glitter waist. We all hoped it would be the first of many flowers and rituals and spring nights with me, back home in Vermillion County.

But at the beginning of that spring semester, before I flew home for Tommy's prom that May, Salem College had broken me. First term had been a wash: My grades were good, but a single room had sent me into a depression. Even though I'd made fast friends that fall on the Gramley third floor, we were weekday buddies bonded by our complaints about the dump we lived in. By Friday lunch, their car keys were in their ignitions, and they were speeding home or to boyfriends' dorm rooms. Salem's reputation as a suitcase college was cemented. That fall, I began going home and spending every weekend with the Lady, friendless and regretting that I hadn't just started my undergrad credits at our community college.

But in December, Jade, a sweet girl from a cute town adjacent to Reidsville, asked me to be her roommate for the spring. It was the lifeline I needed. I accepted, moved one floor down, and began going out with her on the weekends.

Jade and the other girls who lived on Gramley's smoking second floor acted their age: They were reckless and fun, the kind of Salem students who viewed this southern smokestack city as a place to be conquered with menthol cigarettes and vodka. They accepted that Salem was a strange menagerie of smart but broken, empowered but vulnerable women, and they leveraged it. These were brilliant women who excelled at their weekday studies and by Thursday night were ready to get wild. Thursday nights in Winston-Salem were when ladies got into clubs free of charge before midnight and fraternity boys were bored with sleeping with the same girls they sat next to in class.

I'd entered the land of fake IDs (mine gifted by an older classmate) and midnight breakfasts at Mr. Waffle. The girl who gave me the fake ID had my same haircut in the photo but a Mississippi address, which I memorized for the sake of skeptical bouncers and grocery store clerks. I passed effortlessly since these were the days before complex, holographic cards.

The Salem girls took to calling me "Dana Jane." When I started drinking, I was such a lightweight, I couldn't remember my actual (or fake ID) name by the second beer. But my new friends claimed I was the best flirt they'd ever seen. I told them it was as simple as making people feel good. I'd practiced it all my life with King and the Lady.

"She always brings her toys over but won't play with them," my suitemates told a new suitemate to explain my dating habits. They loved to watch me work, they said, coercing frat boys into buying us all Jägermeister and Goldschläger shots that we could down immediately to keep the red Solo cup roofies away. By then, Tommy and I were seeing other people but were still each other's backup plan for his prom and my summers at home. I was untethered and could now enjoy boy flings that never lasted longer than a night out or a week of laptop instant messaging. I was channeling the Lady's transaction-based lifestyle, using men to serve my needs: a pizza delivery boy to cover our late-night food cravings or a lawyer to treat us to an Olive Garden dinner. That semester, second-floor freshmen Gramley women had it all: We were the star students in our seminar classes who booty-dropped in clubs until closing time and had hot, greasy pizza waiting for us when we got back to the dorm.

That semester, my tolerance for alcohol grew, as did my ego and with it my physical body. Drinking in bulk was about control. I thought that if I could outdrink boys at bars and my own Salem girls, I could control my actions and take care of myself and my friends.

I felt freer in my mind when I drank—like I'd found my true self: flirtatious, courageous, bold, tough, uninhibited. When I went out with the Gramley girls, I was the wild girl who kept myself and the group drunk, fed, and entertained. I smoked Marlboro menthols and made it my personal mission to take care of my friends. But the binge-drinking snuck up on my fun-sized frame. I ended up with belly bloat, dopey eyelids, and a neck as thick as a linebacker's, and any liquid courage I'd gained the night before settled in my body and brain like an anvil. Ironically, my attempt at self-mastery led to a total loss of myself.

The following day, I'd attend French class with a migraine, the sweet taste of fermented wheat on my tongue. I ate my way through hangovers at the carb bar at The Rat, filling my plate with pizza and mac 'n' cheese, my blue plastic tumbler spilling over with full-sugar soda. My skinny friends knew better than to reach for the sweets and pasta. But I couldn't stop myself from self-medicating. I was eighteen and on my own, but I was more like my parents than I realized, and I didn't know how to cope. Like King and the Lady, I was always looking for a hit.

After a night out, I was anxious and foggy, worrying about how I'd behaved the night before and whether anyone was talking about me behind my back. A touch of King's paranoia hit me, so over those starch-filled lunch plates, I tried desperately to find my worth in externals, garnering compliments and acceptance and appreciation.

Despite fun Thursday nights out in Winston, life on Salem's campus wasn't collegial. When we weren't drinking, our dorms were home to outbursts from women accusing one another of being fake and manipulative. Single-sex campuses lend themselves to this temperament as well as to the practice of attending classes in pajamas. We acted and looked like Real Housewives who'd recently fired their stylists and surgeons.

Many Salem women—including those who became my closest, lifelong friends—avoided this downward spiral by transferring in droves after their freshman or sophomore year. Those of us who stayed insisted the solution to the drama was the bottle, but that was as short-lived as a clubbing buzz.

Jade transferred after the spring term of our freshman year. The following year, I moved into a suite with girls who would become lifelong friends, but they transferred or opted for early graduation too. I finished my literal "college" sentence at Salem alone. The next academic years, I ran through every clique on campus. With none of my freshman friends left at Salem and knowing that my pajama-clad, reclusive, and depressed mother waited at home, soon I was driving the forty-five minutes to Reidsville every weekend to sit on the Chatmoss couch with the Lady and yell at CNN.

Nearly all Salem classes were seminars. Each session, no more than eight girls sat around a boat of a conference table and bluffed their way through critical thinking.

Week one at Salem, I'd declared two majors and a minor: international relations and French with a political science minor. But my major was swept out from under me when the only political science professor on campus, Dr. Buchanan, awarded me my first-ever C in a mercy killing. He was a Duke PhD who chafed with bitterness at teaching Duke's rejects.

My papers dripped with his frustration: *Repetition. Explain. This makes no sense. You've said this already. Examples. Details. Repetition. Explain. This makes no sense.*

Since he taught every course required for both international relations and political science, I gave up, swapping them both for a history major, with no protest from Dr. Buchanan. My history and French degrees would set me up for law school, which was my singular academic focus once Buchanan dashed my United Nations dream career. I slapped a "Wake Forest University School of Law" sticker on my Corolla and focused my studies on a logical pre-law track: history, with French for fun. I had no aptitude for the latter, but I loved the way the language infiltrated my dreams and rolled off my tongue. And I loved Dr. Etienne, Salem's Mister Rogers of a professor.

Dr. Etienne was a Yale PhD grad who donned the same khaki pants and navy sweater every day. He spoke only French, peering out through greasy glasses from under gray eyebrows as thick as pipe cleaners. He waited patiently for answers to his quick, sharp French, pressing together long string-bean fingers as his eyes shifted to each one of the five of us in his upper-level French seminars. We fumbled our responses, and he politely corrected our misgendering of French nouns.

Dr. Etienne was a full-on hermit with a dash of button-up-shirt bridge troll, and we were certain he lived in Old Salem's well-kept shrubbery that lined Main Hall. We never imagined he had a home and a spouse and offspring until our senior year, when he invited us to his house. Family photos lined the mantel, and the smell of warm food wafted from his wife's cheerful kitchen. He wasn't a recluse; he was just an eccentric-yet-gentle linguaphile.

He and I built a four-year bond between struggling student and exasperated professor. He implored me to try harder, work harder, and make French my focus instead of my hobby.

"*Pauvre ma petite*!" he'd say with sarcasm when I offered him a terrible excuse for missing class or conjugation exercises. His catchphrase didn't translate to anything except "my poor little," but it was his shorthand for feigning pity and calling me out on my equally crappy French.

So I was shocked in the fall of my junior year when I—his party-hard, distracted student—was named the first Etienne French Scholarship recipient of Salem College. The honor came with a country-club dinner with deep-pocket donors. I sweated through my Gap sweater on the drive there, praying I wouldn't have to speak my broken French the entire meal. I was relieved when the benefactor was a jolly bottle blond who just loved Dr. Etienne and champagne.

That scholarship vote of confidence caused me to work harder in French classes even as the LSAT and law school applications awaited.

But the Lady didn't want me to go to law school. "You're not suited for it," she said. "You know what we should do? Visit Duke Divinity School!"

Salem College had a religion course requirement, so I'd taken Eastern Religious Traditions from a Mennonite professor who slipped off his Birkenstocks before he lectured like he was on holy ground. In my mind, religion belonged outside the stacks of the library. I had no interest in pursuing it as a degree. But the Lady clung to the dream that both of her children would graduate from Duke. Even as I took LSAT pretests, she found the one Duke master's program that required no GRE entrance exam score and was likely to accept me with my mediocre Salem grades: the master of divinity.

One late-summer morning before my last year at Salem, we got in the Oldsmobile and drove to Duke's campus. But I was sure I would never go to Duke. I'd given up on them the day I was rejected for their undergraduate class of 2003.

It felt unbearable to visit Duke and get my hopes up. But the Lady convinced me to be open. It wouldn't do any good, she said, to cut the Lord off if he had a plan. Besides, visiting didn't cost anything but time and gas.

Over the phone, I told King about the planned Duke Divinity School visit.

"My Budge—a *Duke* professor. Ain't that something!" King said despite my explanations about being a potential *student,* not a teacher. "I had a veeshun about this."

I saw how pleased both my parents were with the prestige and religion aspects of the Duke possibility, so divinity school became my backup plan, something I'd never planned on doing until that summer.

In tandem with those applications, I had to get my soul right.

Was God really calling me to ministry? Signs come in strange forms, I decided: Childhood near-death experiences. Rock-bottom experiences. Poverty. Middle school fistfights. Bad grades. Addiction. Parents whose manic minds are often more attuned than the rest of ours. Rainbows on the way to the Crystal Cathedral twenty-one years prior. Who was I to tell God how it was all going to shake out?

The Sunday after we visited Duke Divinity School, I made my way down the First Baptist Church Reidsville aisle during the third stanza of "Here I Am, Lord."

Altar calls aren't unusual for Baptists, who rededicate themselves as often as they get a haircut or have a brush with booze or sex. As I headed down the aisle toward Dr. Allan, I wasn't sure what I was going to say. He gave me a Christian side hug at the communion table, leaning his six-foot frame down for me to whisper in his ear: "I think I am called to ministry." He beamed like a little boy who'd just gotten the Christmas gift he'd longed for all year. The hymn finished, and he announced my declaration.

When I got into Duke Divinity School the fall of my senior year at Salem, King and the Lady were prouder than they'd ever been of me, despite knowing I'd never mentioned wanting to be a minister.

"I had a veeshun that this would happen," King insisted.

"My Carolina chaplain!" the Lady said.

She took to calling me "Revy," short for "Reverend," and King managed to work it into the first few seconds of any conversation for the rest of his life.

In their minds, Dr. Schuller's promise had been fulfilled: They'd made the pilgrimage to L.A. and gotten their baby girl, and now they were giving her back to God, like Hannah dedicating her son Samuel back to the Lord in the Old Testament.

What was left of my Salem clique attended my ordination, snickering at ritual and refusing to eat the homemade lunch the fine Baptist women had prepared.

The next Thursday night, I accompanied the same girls to the Tap Room, where we got drunk and smoked Marlboro

Lights. My suitemates told every man in the bar I was a Southern Baptist minister just to see how they'd react. They bought us all shots.

My senior year, I lived a double life: reverend, admitted to Duke Divinity School, enmeshed with my mother, engaged in suitemate drama, and hungry for men. Fall semester, I accepted Adderall when anyone offered it and stole it when they didn't. Though I was still vehemently against illegal drugs, I justified prescriptions—even when they weren't mine.

When I suspected a friend had done lines of blow with a man who'd slept in her room the night before, I licked my fingers and picked up the residue off the floor just because it was there. Snorting it would have been out of the question, as would smoking the joints my friends snuck as we sat in dry showers and giggled at how we'd survived four years of the absurdities of single-sex education. But checking the purity after the fact? That was fine. It was bitter, exactly how I felt inside.

Christmas of my junior year—just eleven months before my ordination—I parked a fifth of Kahlúa liquor on the Chatmoss kitchen counter. The brown-and-yellow bottle was next to the coffeepot, like a shrine to a long-ago tropical vacation. The sun wasn't even up when I poured three tablespoons into my Folgers like it was half-and-half.

It was rare that anyone brought booze into Chatmoss. Evelyn, my devil-chasing Southern Baptist maternal grandmother, would rather have died *again* than witness me drinking hair-of-the-dog coffee. And surely my mother, who was raised in a farmhouse drier than grits, found it unsettling. At the very least she found it weak, like I wasn't doing my part to direct all my mental and physical energy into anticipating and serving her needs. The Trent family had been breastfed on the Baptist warnings that alcohol could ruin your reputation. Concerns over its effects on your body, mind, and spirit were second to concerns over your standing. Trent offspring knew that it took no more than two busybodies to start a telephone tree and spread the word all over town that you'd been seen in the ABC parking lot and thus were hitting the sauce. My mother was so averse to drinking that she referred to it only in clinical terms, as in "ETOH," the acronym for *ethyl alcohol.* "Such a shame," she'd say, crossing out faces in the church directory with a red pen and writing "ETOH!"

The only whiskey I saw in my mother's possession was never consumed. She kept a single shot of Canadian Club as old as the Kennedy administration in a plastic flask hidden deep in her American Tourister luggage. The pain pills, benzos, and uppers were always strewn about: in nightstands, in filing cabinets, in kitchen cabinets, on counters, and in purses. But when it came to "ETOH!" she was wound tighter than the Puritans.

"No-good alkie," the Lady called our Ninth Street trailer neighbor Boozy Piddler. She and King looked down their noses at BP and anyone who lacked the discipline to lay off the perfectly legal sauce.

So I knew that bringing home a bottle of liquor was bolder than a neon Vegas sign. I'd spent years using my fake ID to supply my suitemates with a Lake Mead's worth of Arbor Mist. The disposable-camera photos of my bloated body downing shots of milky nectar are proof that I was in deep.

I think I'd imagined then that the Kahlúa would rile the Lady up. Would she stomp around our dirty apartment and scrawl "ETOH!" on headshots of me? It was my rebellion against Salem and leaving Vermillion County.

But she said nothing.

"I think I need to go to rehab," I said, taking a sip of coffee.

"Don't be ridiculous," she said. "You don't need rehab."

I slurped my sauce, trying to prove my point.

The Lady wasn't fazed. The decades she'd spent trying to rewire her unquiet mind had been the best years of her life. Each bedridden major depression and suicide attempt was followed by a stay at her version of the Ritz.

"It was a vacation," she'd say, pining for the inpatient psychiatric stints in Ohio and North Carolina, where she'd been comatose with sedatives before analysis.

"We had the best time," the Lady would say of her months locked in a ward, "except when I threw a pillow at Dr. Hines. He was furious with me!" She laughed. "Did I tell you about the time Clark and I signed out to go to the Blockade Runner at the beach?" She smiled. "We sure fooled them—just went to the other side of campus." She sighed like a middle-aged woman flipping through her high school yearbook.

"I think I need rehab," I said again.

"Don't be so dramatic!" the Lady said, sitting on our hand-me-down couch in a pink bathrobe, her irritation hidden behind *Rich Dad, Poor Dad* as James Taylor played on our Bose stereo, which had survived the bankruptcy.

"Wouldn't you just love a fresh cup of coffee?" she redirected, moving her cup from behind the dog-eared pages.

"Do *you* want more coffee?" I asked her.

"Does a wildcat live in the woods?" she replied, and I peeled myself off the couch to grab her mug.

"Pretty is as pretty does," she said.

So I kept drinking. My body grew as bloated as a holiday

float, red and puffy from the vicious cycle of binge-boozing, hangovers, and unlimited carbs.

By the time I was a senior, four years of undergraduate turmoil culminated in the events that led to my being banned from my own dorm room. My current clique had attended my ordination, poking fun at my apparently newfound religious fanaticism. But they didn't know that I'd been conceived under the auspices of my parents' belief in Dr. Schuller's California miracles. They didn't know that I'd grown up with Tammy Faye and Dana Community Bible Church and the First Baptist youth group and a cult-leader-turned-rabbi father who cast "veeshuns" for his disciples and blessed inanimate objects with greasy palms.

That December, it got so cold at Salem that the rain turned to ice. We watched as frozen tree limbs fell and electricity flickered off and on. Faculty and dining hall staff were sent home. Bored and hungry seniors took to the basement of Bidding, our dorm, for nature-induced senior revelry, an ice-storm last hurrah of on-campus indoor smoking, drinking, and partying. It was two weeks after my Southern Baptist ordination.

The ice-storm party is a blurry mental Polaroid in which I can't distinguish villains from heroes, but what I know for sure is that it resulted in my exile from campus. Not in an official way because of rule breaking, but rather through ostracism by the peers I trusted. My remaining Salem friends were rich women poised to conquer the world come graduation in May. They'd be off to run corporations and host galas, marry up and cherish wealth like it was a blood type they had to pass on. I stood no chance in a game like that. But my mistake was not having self-acceptance.

We were all gathered in the Bidding basement for this last

hurrah, nineties hip-hop blasting alongside mixed drinks and Marlboros. I fished in my purse for my ChapStick but couldn't find it. Half-drunk, I muttered that my mother must have taken it out. The room fell silent.

"Your *mother* took it out?" someone said.

I nodded. Sure, of course, she cleaned my purse out for me.

The party halted like I'd just said, "And that's when I tossed that baby right into the dumpster."

Why wouldn't my mother have access to my purse? I wondered. I was twenty-one and thought it normal for someone to dump the contents of a woman's purse onto the floor to examine, cull, and take what they deemed valuable. I had no sense of boundaries.

Here, at a college party, the purse debacle turned into a slurred intervention. It had probably been festering behind my back for weeks. Sitting on a lumpy couch, I left my body when the girls piled on that I was too old to let my mother go through my purse and, furthermore, they'd noticed my unhealthy relationship with her, spouting expensive terms they'd learned in Psychology 101 like *enmeshed, entanglement,* and *co-dependent.*

The incident broke one of my unspoken rules: *Do not acknowledge that anything is wrong with my parents or my relationship with them. Everything is fine.* But the drawback to an upbringing with a schizophrenic father and a mother with personality disorders is that until I developed my own healthy coping skills to deal with heightened emotions, I relied on my brain's go-to defense mechanisms birthed straight from the Ninth Street trailer. Would I explode as King had taught me and defend my mother's honor, reaching for the slender white necks of everyone in the room? Would I play the victim, cry and beg, like the Lady had taught me, manipulating them into acceptance and forgiveness? Or would I just shrink and shut up and hit the booze?

The Salem women pitied me. I pitied myself. They saw me as an immature child who vacillated between Southern Baptist minister and twenty-one-year-old life of the party. I was insincere and inauthentic, they said, wearing a mask, covering up my crazy family and my own crazy insides. In a way, they were right. But I wasn't ready to face that, understand that, take responsibility for it, and live my own life.

I couldn't run. Had North Carolina not been blanketed in several inches of ice, I'd have packed my Corolla and gotten the hell out of there, rushing home to the Lady. As it was, I considered taking my chances, risking a car accident that would leave me dead or at least with a broken leg. *That would show them,* I thought.

Instead, I was their captive audience in their version of the hot box all night. What began as an ice-storm party became a list of all their grievances in the time they'd known me. One big issue was the Lady's presence on the Salem College campus. It was nothing for my mother to come stay at Salem for a week at a time, holed up in the Alumni House guest room right across from our dorm. I'd trot back and forth between my suitemates and her, thinking nothing of it. *The best of both worlds,* I told myself: family time in which I was the Lady's Revy and party time in which I was Dana Jane, the fun-loving purveyor of boys and free shots.

But I'd miscalculated the balance in my Salem friends' bank account. Transactional relationships work well until they don't; I'm usually the first to overdraw. My annoying people-pleasing, love addiction, and childlike neediness had pushed the relationships to the breaking point. Superficial intrigue and flirtation go only so far before people want honest and self-sufficient adult friends. I was just a hair-pulling, food and love and booze addict with a compulsive need for external affirmation while still attached to her mother's umbilical cord.

I nodded and cried, absorbing everything they told me and vowing to change. Then I packed my bags as soon as the ice thawed.

Back in Reidsville, I gave the Lady a play-by-play of the ice-storm intervention.

Mom said to ignore them. "Give them a rope," she said. "They'll hang themselves."

A college friend did, in fact, hang herself not too long after.

"Told ya," the Lady said when I heard the news. I was stunned by her coldness and her prophecy.

I'd hoped that the frenzy of exams and the pause of Christmas break would alleviate the Salem crisis. But I miscalculated again.

Over Christmas break, my Bidding roommate sent me a terse email asking me not to return to our shared dorm room. By January, I'd been made into what the Lewman family called a "sacrificial lamb," a pushed-out pawn in a chess game. A beat-down dog, King called it.

I could barely sleep. I kept having a recurring dream. I was at Salem College graduation that May but hadn't completed the courses I needed to walk. "You're missing credits," the registrar told me in the dream. Her face was gaunt like a Halloween mask.

The Lady shrugged it off. "You've faced worse," she said. Even so, the nightly dream told me my bachelor's degree was still in limbo, and I couldn't get into Duke until I completed it.

The nightmare persisted for more than a decade after my Salem College graduation—and even after my Duke graduation.

At the actual Salem ceremony, we sat in alphabetical order, and I was next to women I barely knew. My friends put their arms around one another for photos. Graduation marked one of the loneliest days in my twenty-two years of life—I was almost as isolated as I'd been during the Lady's Baylor night shift at Duke. Lee and his family attended. He and the Lady made up for it with sweets and gifts and love, but I could tell they were troubled. In the sea of happy women wearing grad caps marked with our next destinations, mine read, "Duke Div." I wasn't going to law school. And I never saw anyone I graduated with that year from Salem again. I kept up only with the girls from spring semester of freshman year—the ones who transferred when they saw the Salem scribble on the wall.

Duke Divinity School was full of students who had just wrapped up religion degrees at Harvard and Princeton and Yale with more academics than finishing-school drama. They knew hefty theological doctrines and read *The Brothers Karamazov* for fun. That first semester, I nearly drowned in New Testament and Early Church History.

Durham housing was expensive. I rented an attached mother-in-law suite in a gender studies professor's home my first year. Before my second year, I told the Lady we should combine households and get an apartment together in Chapel Hill at Glen Lennox, where we'd lived for several months when I was eleven and she was going through bankruptcy. I lived on my own only that first year.

I suspected that the Lady was dying of depression in Reidsville.

During the three years I spent at Duke, I didn't drink. I swapped booze with food and ballooned to 170 pounds, unrecognizable in my five-foot frame.

The chicken-or-egg psychology of being an obese person is perplexing. At age twenty-five, my joints ached from the extra weight, so I didn't want to move or exercise, which piled on the weight. Food is a quick upper and fix for what troubles you, until you begin slathering cream cheese icing on saltines at 8:00 A.M., which I did every day. Muffins weren't tasty without eight pats of butter; an evening at home with the Lady wasn't complete without fresh chocolate chip cookies.

My second year at Duke, G&GL both died within three months of each other, Grandmother in September and Grandfather in December. They were just shy of sixty years of marriage. I was so consumed with parsing Greek verbs and reading five books a week that I hardly had time to fly home. I processed their deaths by eating more.

King processed their deaths by cashing checks. He felt he was finally free of them, unencumbered by their judgment, their abuse, and the burden of living in Vermillion County under their watchful eye. But I suspected he loved and grieved them more than he wanted to admit. Instead, King spouted that he had waited for the moment he'd get to count Grandfather's money with all ten of his own fingers. That time had finally come.

My father bought a brand-new trailer and five acres with their cash. Nestled in the country, his new place was minutes from the American Legion. By then, he'd become proud of his military service—even calling himself a veteran and carrying his VA card with him. The benefit of reclaiming his troubled marine years was the benefits themselves—VA medical insurance and services and paid-for healthcare. He still wasn't able to collect any social security since he hadn't fully paid in with forty quarters, but now he had G&GL's money, which was slowly running out.

We'd rekindled our relationship again. It suffered at the beginning of college, when Tommy and I broke up and I moved through a series of strange decisions to distance myself from Vermillion County, including changing my surname from Lewman to Trent and even canceling summer plane tickets G&GL sent me for weeks-long visits. I was pulling away from them because it made the Lady's depression lighter. But that was only temporary.

When the Lady and I moved in together my second year at Duke, I began to realize her problems weren't environmental. I thought it had been Indiana. Or homelessness. Or Chapel Hill apartments and Reidsville. It turned out that no matter where the Lady landed, she was miserable. And she loved company in her misery.

After I nearly dropped out from academic overwhelm that first semester at Duke, the Lady insisted I go to a fancy Duke psychiatrist she'd known when she was a Baylor nurse. Expecting a significant diagnosis, the Lady was disappointed when he suggested I was going through what all Duke graduate students go through: panic, anxiety, and the depression that comes from being overloaded with courses at one of the most rigorous universities in the nation. It was temporary, he suggested, and prescribed me Lexapro to help me make it through three divinity school years.

Not long after G&GL died, my regular practitioner added a Klonopin prescription for acute anxiety to the mix. I began taking it excessively, convinced I had the same panic attack and major depressive disorder as my mother. It pleased the Lady to know we were "in the same boat." She wasn't happy unless she was "needed" by the "mentally ill." The more anxiety and depression I exhibited, the more elated she became. It was a shift from the Dr. Gloria days when the Lady hoped I wasn't "psychotic like your father." Somehow, anxiety and depression were acceptable mental illnesses; psychosis was not.

My Klonopin misuse during those years came to a head when I took too much before leading a church service as an intern. Words slurring into each other like trombone notes, I stumbled over prayers and scripture. The congregation just thought I was sleep-deprived. But the Lady knew.

"Well, I don't want you looking foolish," she said at our favorite Chinese lunch place. My embarrassment was hers. Reputation was still everything to my mother.

But she was never ashamed of therapy. Duke offered free counseling services to its students, most of whom were so driven and perfectionistic that earning an A- on a calculus exam would trigger suicidal ideation. I had my own ideations, but they were prompted by befuddlement with subjects I didn't yet understand—theology, Greek, and Hebrew. My psychologist, Dr. Cameron, and I met on Fridays. He reminded me of Dr. Etienne, with his lanky build and dark blue wool sweaters. He yawned during our sessions, bored with my self-indulgent pessimism.

Not to be outdone in the department of mental illness, the Lady returned to intensive weekly therapy at the UNC Adult Psychiatry Clinic. While she fawned over her doctors and dogged the "undesirables" and "no-goods" in waiting rooms and group therapy sessions, Dr. Cameron taught me techniques I used. I joined Weight Watchers for my food addiction, my love addiction quieted with abstinence and daily cognitive behavioral journaling practices, and my compulsive hair pulling was traded for obsessive cleaning, a coping technique that proved beneficial to me, even if annoying to others.

Despite Dr. Cameron's cognitive behavioral therapy tools, my graduation from Duke Divinity School intensified my enmeshment with the Lady. While other twenty-five-year-olds were sorting out their careers and life partners, I was doubling down on my efforts to take care of my mother. I never felt confident that the Lady could live on her own, a feeling she said was projection. Maybe it was.

The Lady continued therapy, as she had off and on since her father committed suicide when she was nineteen. Even as I hoped her sessions would make her more outgoing, less negative, and less dependent on the filing cabinet full of anti-depressants, anti-anxiety pills, and pain meds, her mental illness got worse. A year after I graduated, her depression was the worst I'd seen. Her eyes were as empty as a freshly dug grave, and she was confined to bed. I signed her up for free grief counseling with a local hospice to supplement her meds and UNC therapy, and I offered to organize an inpatient hospitalization.

"Those aren't what they used to be," the Lady said. "The service is terrible now." She scoffed, like it had been downgraded to a three-star hotel. By "service," she meant the inpatient psychiatric staff.

"And I don't want to be around those no-goods," she added. "So uncouth!"

By "no-goods," she meant the psychotic, suicidal addicts and teens that were now held for seventy-two hours at the local hospital. Gone were her glory days of the three-month stint at Duke with Freudian and Jungian chauvinist white male doctors who doped up patients for a week, then analyzed them when they came out of their comas. Now it was young women and men running the show with practical, evidence-based skills training like cognitive behavioral and dialectical behavioral therapy that put the responsibility back on patients to help take charge of rewiring their own brains.

This bothered the Lady, who was keen on intellectualizing psychiatry without implementing its practical tools. Her depression worsened that year, and I spent hours at her bedside trying to find a fix. It arrived—or so I thought—in a nugget from her past: a beef with a former therapist in Cincinnati. His treatment of her had been questionable but likely not entirely his fault, given his patient's mercurial nature. Still, she wanted his license revoked.

"If it will help you get better, I will help you figure it out," I said and spent the next year sorting through the bureaucratic tape of the Ohio Board of Psychology. Letters and audiotape depositions followed. My life became a 24/7 cycle of meeting the Lady's needs.

King spent the last five years of his life in Vermillion County, in that squeaky new trailer bought with Grandfather's money. Age, it turned out, spurred a desire to find new poisons. King was weary of navigating the market of grams and kilos and quarters and pounds. His attentiveness had thinned as rapidly as his hair, and he no longer had the sharpness required to buy an eight ball of coke. So he drank.

It isn't lost on me that my father and I both landed there, deep in the booze and trying to find our way out. But for the three of us—King, the Lady, and now an adult version of me—old baggage was hard to let go of, no matter where we found ourselves living, no matter how new our paths looked. King had his new place on an old coal pile; I had my new master's degree from an old university. But we were still us: Vermillion County drug-running trailer trash one meth hit away from the carny caste.

ELEVEN

The Death of a King

W ITH G&GL GONE, KING SETTLED IN AT THE COUNTRY bars back home in Indiana, and the Lady and I lived together back in Glen Lennox. I was in my late twenties and assumed this was how my life would continue on. I imagined we'd all live out our days like this: in our silos, drowning in booze and prescriptions and sadness. But there is something subtle about the power of therapy, at least for me: Its usefulness sneaks up on you when you least expect it. A coping mechanism or a reframing rushes to the front, and you find yourself healthier, inch by inch.

The Thanksgiving after my twenty-seventh birthday, I started online dating. I was obese and had barely kicked my affinity for binge-drinking followed by Klonopin. My brain felt free from the cotton-ball numbing anti-depressants and anti-anxiety meds, and I was working as a secretary at Duke Divinity School. After I finished Duke in 2006, I spent a year as an end-of-life care resident chaplain on one of UNC's intensive care units. The position was term-limited, and while it was meaningful to sit with patients at the end of their lives, it was exhausting. When the residency concluded in 2007, the Great Recession was underway and full-time jobs were hard to come by. The secretary gig fell into my lap. It was decent employment when there was none to be had, but my pride told me it was humiliating. My student loans had to be deferred when my paycheck barely covered the rent the Lady and I owed. Rather than working as a graduate-degree theologian and human with dignity, I spent my lunch hours sobbing in the Duke Chapel pews.

Then I met Fred, my future husband, that Christmas: a surprise the Lady didn't anticipate or approve of. "I won't get married" had been my mantra since Salem College. It was a clever way of pushing potential relationships away before I could feel the pinch of rejection. But something—I don't know what: maybe therapy, maybe divinity—nudged me to try eHarmony.

Fred and I were engaged one year later.

The Lady was devastated.

But she knew I'd go through with it. So, she insisted on being the parental star of the wedding.

"Close only counts in horseshoes and hand grenades," the Lady had said when I told her I was *close* to deciding about whether to uninvite King to the July wedding. That's when I wrote the letter. Appeasing my mother was something I'd mastered by then. I didn't realize that no matter how hard I tried to meet her needs, it would never be enough.

From the geographical distance to the name change, by the time I was twenty-nine, the Lady had finally worn me down enough to convince me that it was time to cut off Vermillion County. This was a glorious moment for my mother, who'd won the battle all unhealthy divorcés fight: Which parent will the child ultimately choose? Because they believe that, at their core, children experiencing the sting of their parents' separation can't possibly choose both. Someone must be the enemy. And the Lady's villainous traits were easily hidden compared with schizophrenia like King's, which is, by nature, not an inconspicuous disease. Personality disorders like my mother's—with their mania or depression or anxiety—show up as patterns over time, subtle and artful, such that you don't realize you're bleeding until decades later, hand to your slit throat, unable to shout in protest.

That's how I came to write the letter. I was finally choosing between being King's Vermillion County daughter and the Lady's Southern Baptist minister:

December 2, 2009

Dear Dad:

My upcoming wedding is the launch of my new life with Fred. For this occasion, it's imperative that I honor myself and the life I've built in North Carolina. I feel that your presence at our wedding would be very difficult for me.

Since 1987, I've been raised by one parent. I know you've attempted to heal the subsequent rifts of divorce and abandonment in your own way. However, our rare visits and weekly phone calls do not repair the twenty-two-year chasm between us.

Your behaviors over the years have been hurtful and painful to me. I have felt shame, embarrassment, loneliness, and estrangement as a result of my

*feelings. I do not want to experience these feelings
on my very special day. I am asking you not to attend my wedding.*

I trust you understand my decision.

Dana

That letter was what King called a "Jewish death," or
"JD" for short. It was like an Amish shunning and it was not
an actual practice of Judaism but was his way of noting when
people cut him off or he cut them off. He'd been on the giving
or receiving end of many JDs, including with his youngest
brother, Boot, whom he hated more than anyone else in the
world.

"Jewish death! Jewish death! You've got to give them the
Jewish death! JD. JD 'em!" he'd taught me. The advice was
usually given during my summers in Indiana, when I told him
about unrequited teenage love, or later when I told him over
the phone about my senior year falling-out with my Salem
schoolmates.

But the letter was the first time I'd put my own feelings (at
least I thought they were my own) before a parent's. It was
also the first time I used my "voice" in writing. But in doing
so, I was employing the very tactic I'd learned from two way-
ward parents who'd cut and run whenever things got too
complicated. They cast away jobs and relationships, ditching
life's version of itchy wool sweaters. I wasn't good at conflict—
the Lady's, King's, or my own. I was programmed to explode
or stonewall. I'd spent decades sitting in my parents' distress:
depression, anxiety, hallucinations, and hatred for each other
"cured" only with amphetamines and benzos and pain pills
and booze and weed and white. I learned to shut up and be

quiet, dismiss my own misery. Whatever it was in their brain chemistry and childhoods that made them unable to cope with the disquiet of their minds, I'd absorbed like a teacher's pet. So, in the letter, I *thought* I was standing up for myself. In reality, I was swinging the pendulum too far, a perfect storm having led up to the moment I dropped it in the mailbox.

Nine months prior to the day I mailed it, I'd quit the secretary job and landed my first professional writing job. It wasn't glamorous; I wasn't a journalist. I was a low-level communications executive hired to write fundraising copy for a nonprofit. I spent my days in a dark office, piecing together testimonials of children and parents affected by trauma. I parsed research and learned how to explain evidence-based practices to laypeople like me. It was triggering to learn of a world I never knew existed: kids and parents who admitted they'd been hurt and were learning to trade chaos for calm.

I sat in meeting after meeting with fancy nonprofit psychologists who told these troubling stories—and how their federal research dollars were helping develop treatments to put these children (and their families) back on track to whatever a new "normal" might be. The more I heard, the more it felt like home. I recognized the narrative as my own, the symptoms as layers of my neuroses: my addictions, my anxiety, my tendencies, my coping mechanisms.

A few months after taking the job, I began having intrusive thoughts about the traumatic events from my childhood. I realized I was not just the storyteller at work but one of the characters in the drama.

At the time, I was in therapy with Dr. Cameron, prattling on about problems that I now realize were more about enmeshment with my mentally ill parents and less about real mental illness present in me. My anxiety and depression worsened; I was consumed with the well-being of my parents, mostly the Lady. I realized this only because when my parents disappeared, so did my symptoms.

Dr. Cameron suggested EMDR (Eye Movement Desensitization and Reprocessing), a modality in which the patient recalls specific traumatic events while shifting their eyes from side to side in order to remap or rewire that neural pathway.

Ties with King had become strained because of the Lady. By the time I was engaged, she and I had been living together as adults for six years. I was wrapping up my twenties and searching for my adult identity, putting myself back together after the Salem College rejection and alienation, and incessantly trying to fix her. When my parents got divorced, the Lady painted King as a psychotic con artist. She was right, but she failed to take responsibility for her own actions: how she'd contributed to the crumbling of the relationship between two mentally ill healthcare professionals that began in a psychiatric hospital of all places—a coupling doomed from the beginning.

The letter to King felt impulsive, but it was years in the making. The Lady had been yearning for my father's own "Jewish death." She'd grown resentful of my ties to Vermillion County, my affection for G&GL, Aunt Marietta, Uncle Leuge, Lindah, and Doggy. She never liked Tommy, and she sure as hell didn't want anything to do with King. She often interrupted my Sunday night phone calls with him, saying she had something urgent she needed me to do. At the ten-minute mark, she'd tap her invisible wristwatch and usher me off the phone.

Instead of speaking with my father about my confusion, my trauma work, my feelings, my troubles, and, most of all, my anger, I "slit his throat," just the way I'd seen both my parents do to others and the way they'd taught me to do. Instead of asserting my need to be heard and seen—to be needy or a "burden" or an actual *child* of my parents—I burned the relationship with King to the ground. My explosive upbringing and stuffed, internalized rage and pain had turned into maladaptive coping, for which I took no responsibility.

I wrote the letter for two reasons: first, to please my mother, and second, because I was eager to avoid confrontation and embarrassment at my upcoming nuptials. Would King's incurable schizoaffective disorder cause him to show up in overalls? Would guests gasp at this knife-brandishing, paranoid cult leader who cast "veeshuns" and spoke in Levitical law? But I later wondered, *What would or could have happened if I'd just been direct with him about it all?*

Looking back, I realize the letter was an attempt at what I thought was integration: Could I fully embody what I thought was my own ideal self (strongly influenced by my mother's ideals)—a southern, polite, people-pleasing, finishing-school-educated minister—if I just erased King from my past? I'd finally become *Reverend,* a Duke graduate, and no one needed to know I'd been a manipulative drunk with a food and pill addiction. I'd found a good, religious man who loved me. Extreme poverty, suicidal threats, abuse, and hustling no longer filled my days. Budgie and her razor blades were buried in the Indiana cornfields.

I revoked my father's wedding invitation on December 2, 2009. We never spoke again. One month before my wedding, he died.

If my crystal ball hadn't been broken that week, I would have placed that letter in a drawer, called him, and let it be.

King will outlive us all, I'd thought. He'd laughed in the devil's face so many times before. I thought back to the suicide threat in the Ninth Street trailer when I visited him.

Back then, I'd thought, *If I leave him, he will die. It will be my fault.*

Now I thought, *I left him and he did die. It is my fault.*

The next few weeks were a blur. My fiancé, Fred, went with me to the Vermillion County funeral. The wedding frenzy was put on hold as we flew across the country to bury King.

Regret is the sharpest emotion because there are no takebacks in this lifetime. This isn't a dress rehearsal. I'd gambled with my father's life, and I'd lost. The pain was as heavy as the granite tombstone we picked out the day after we put him in the ground. We engraved it with an image of an open Bible and "The King."

"Here. Your dad's things," Uncle Leuge said when Fred and I arrived. We stood in his kitchen at the Lewman Museum around the same table where we'd spent hours hearing Vermillion County stories, including the one about the grate over what had allegedly been the Underground Railroad. Leuge handed me the plastic baggie King kept as his wallet. Billfolds were for rich people, my father had always said. Sandwich bags as flimsy as limp linguini were what King relied on. If they were good enough to keep an hour's worth of weed hidden until you smoked it, they were good enough to keep an afternoon's worth of money in your pocket until you spent it. King liked to know his assets at a glance.

My father's VA ID card was on top. He looked stern, upset that they'd made him take his photo without his signature Yankees hat. His Friar Tuck cue-ball head was wild with stringy black hair on the sides, like Bozo the Clown met Just for Men in midnight black.

A tarnished pocket crucifix like the ones glued to all those dashboards was pressed against an appointment reminder and his license. Leuge handed me King's worn handkerchief, a relic of being raised by World War II parents who didn't touch a Kleenex until their sixties. I lifted the bandana to my face: It smelled like Old Spice, marijuana skunk, and Vaseline.

The next day, good midwestern devotees with street names like Pyro Pete, Saltlick, Devil Killer, and Meatsweat flocked to Dana Community Bible Church. Their devotion was as strong as the cigarette stench that filled the pews. Vermillion County residents arrived by the hundreds in the tiny town of Dana, the site of Tiger's hanging, the boys' beatings, revenge on bullies, electric fences, and fiery alleys where deputies were stoned.

Friendship was King's highest virtue. His life was full of gangs and good buddies. Had I learned to embrace him as a friend, I could have been his daughter.

We opened his casket. Dressed in the pinstripe "rabbinical suit" he'd stolen from his father and never returned, he lay there with his beard long and curly and neatly trimmed above his crossed arms. Grandmother, had she been living, may have even approved. It was the same beard they'd fought over and the same suit he'd worn when he'd duct-taped tens of thousands of dollars to himself in the 1980s when he said the feds had followed him off international flights. He'd always slept in the dusty cornfields across from the Ninth Street trailer. At dawn, he'd crawl under the skirting and through the rat-recliner trapdoor in the kitchen of our trailer. I wondered if anyone had had that suit dry-cleaned.

King commanded a crowd, even in rest.

The finality of it smothered me. I hadn't expected my father's end to arrive in this way: a cardiac arrest on a June day, alone in his trailer until Saltlick dropped by. He'd come over to mow King's weeds.

King's youngest brother, Boot, had heard about the funeral. Just before the service, he sauntered in. My father's entourage moved to the edge of their pews, muscles tense. Uncle Boot processed up the church aisle like the pope. He approached the casket and we all collectively gasped. Gang members tapped their pockets, prepared to slit a throat if they needed to. Everyone sitting in Dana Community Bible Church was uncertain what Boot had come for. King's hatred of his baby brother was no secret—thousands in Vermillion County had heard my father snarl "Booty-Boy" with the same disdain with which he said "Cocksucker!" to every cop he ever saw. I suspect we all thought Boot would spit on King or choke him, cracking his rigor-mortis limbs like candy canes.

But Boot *knelt* at the casket, slid his fat hand into King's coffin, and placed *something* on the pillowy white lining. Was it a grenade?

Uncle Leuge interrupted Boot's feigned reverence with a throat-clearing sign that the service was beginning. King's youngest brother took his seat as we all strained our necks to discern what he'd placed in my father's final resting bed.

On the way to the gravesite, Leuge pulled a giant coin out from under King's head. No one could decipher its significance.

King's grave is just south of Dana, Indiana. He was buried with military honors including a twenty-one-gun salute and a flag-covered casket.

While we waited for the preacher to usher folks into the little limestone chapel at Bono Cemetery, I introduced Fred to Pyro Pete, King's good buddy.

Dad's death brought out everyone's sentimental side. As

sniffling grown men wiped their noses with hands as big as bear paws, Pyro Pete put his digits on Fred's shoulder and looked him right in the eye. "If you ever hurt her, I'll kill you," Pyro Pete told him. He took a draw on his generic cigarette and waited for Fred to acknowledge the message.

More nervous than I'd ever seen him, my fiancé nodded and winced when Pyro Pete slapped his shoulder with a "Glad we have an understanding."

In that moment, I realized for the first time that King—or his reputation for crazy—wasn't around to protect me and that maybe he hadn't been the one protecting us all along after all. King's Vermillion County good buddies knew how sick he was. There wasn't much anyone could have done for him on the mental-illness side except look out for his family and keep rivals away. They gave him rides when he was wild with paranoia and hid his money for him when he showed up with bands of cash taped to his chest. They consoled him when he swore the feds had bugged his single wide. Food showed up on our doorstep when all we had to eat were ketchup sandwiches.

I'd been raised by these Vermillion County folks: King's disciples, G&GL, Aunt Marietta, Uncle Leuge. They were my angels when my parents were unable to take care of us. And I hadn't even known it.

At the end of the graveside service, King was lowered into the ground where cornfields grow as far as the eye can see. As much as I wanted to feel elated, I felt empty. King had been invincible—immortal, eternally young, fueled by a life of illegal uppers and downers, shirking any responsibility that sought to tie him down. Because he'd already lived so long and so hard, it seemed impossible that his heart had failed him at just sixty-three. He'd defied the odds time after time:

gang fights and draft dodging, grand jury indictments and cross-country benders, hearse driving and kiddie-ride trafficking. Crime, poverty, drugs, and his enemies hadn't killed him. How had we ended up here?

I was stiff with grief.

After the service, we made our way back down Main Street, crossing the railroad track into town just like Lindah, Doggy, and I had thousands of times before on King's midnight bike rides through Dog Town.

In the Dana volunteer firehouse across from the church, we sat at folding tables and remembered the hours we spent jitterbugging on that same concrete floor with "Judy Bags." Hundreds had gathered for the church-sponsored lunch, and we ate and laughed and told King stories for thirty minutes. Then Boot burst through the side door of the firehouse, wearing a neon trucker's hat but still in his funeral suit. He held a portable karaoke machine. Everyone looked up from their fried chicken. Boot turned on the amp and began speaking. "My brother was a prophet," he said. No one could make out his next sentence because the crowd collectively cranked up their polite reception conversations to a roar. Defeated, he turned off his amp and sat down to pick at his bird carcass.

On those hot June days that bookended the funeral, Fred and I cleaned out King's single wide, the brand-new bachelor-pad-turned-dump he'd bought for cash with his inheritance from G&GL.

From the springs-only mattress he'd destroyed in his search for government bugs to the porn hidden in his closet, nothing had changed. King was still paranoid, schizophrenia still haunting him. Fred and I tore the trailer apart like two criminals, looking for cash and drugs. Saltlick told us King's "papers" were in there somewhere—a deed to the place—but

I knew better. The only "papers" my father kept were stacks of cash and the same JOB cigarette-rolling papers he'd used when I was a kid. So we pulled pre-fab panels off walls and checked the spaces behind the water heater, searching for pieces of him. His King James Bible, well worn and grayed with ashes, was still on the trailer counter. Like in the Ninth Street single wide where he'd trained me, King's "office" kitchen cabinets were stuffed with stained and dirty papers. Only this time, the military system had been providing him a steady stream of healthcare. My father's diagnoses, listed in black and white—schizophrenia, schizoaffective disorder, hepatitis C, insomnia, cirrhosis of the liver, osteoarthritis—afforded him the prescription medication that eased his suffering in those last five years. Empty pain pill bottles filled days before his death were the only drugs we found. He'd either cleaned up or been cleaned out.

Saltlick and Devil Killer dropped by to say hi. They hugged us in the weeds they had mowed the day Saltlick discovered King's unconscious body inside.

"I don't know what happened," Saltlick said, referring to my wedding. "But King was coming to your wedding."

"He was gonna be there," Devil Killer added with the slow drawl he'd always had.

TWELVE

Vermillion

NEVER IMAGINED I'D BE AN ORPHAN.

I pictured my final days shuffling scrambled eggs on bed trays to both my parents. Gray-haired and hunched over, they'd sit while I changed their TV channels to Dr. Schuller reruns. The worn Bibles on their nightstands would be open to King's Levitical law and the Lady's Gospels—ready for me to place glasses over my dimming eyes and read to them aloud. I'd take care of them until my death, I thought, which I was certain would come before theirs.

The Lady was relieved by King's disappearance. In her mind, he'd been the ball and chain that had caused all her later-life problems, from the financial burdens of bankruptcy to the arthritis in her knees and back.

Her elation didn't last long. When my wedding day arrived, she popped so many Ritalin that she moved in twitches and jerks like a scared squirrel. I picked out her outfit and did her makeup.

She walked me down the aisle.

"Worst day of my life," she told me later, sipping her coffee.

My brother Lee and his wife bought her a condo overlooking a pool she never used. She had daydreams of swimming before dawn and after dusk, but other people interrupted those plans. Shared spaces baffled her; children and adults were too loud or too uncouth for her taste. Before she stopped driving, she spent her days shopping with credit cards, attending therapy appointments, and begging me to make the thirty-minute trek to come spend the night with her. When I did, I was back in servant mode, tidying up and cooking and changing sheets and cleaning bathrooms and vacuuming and sorting weeks' worth of psychiatric meds. Even in her old age, she was skilled at building and lounging in a bed nest.

With each year that I stayed married, the Lady grew angrier and sicker. Her mental health declined as rapidly as her diseases escalated. She began to cut ties with loved ones, stamping King's "Jewish death" on relatives and friends whom she perceived as having done her wrong. Just as she marked yearbooks and church directories with "ETOH," she added other offenses to the list like "from the North" and "talks about themselves."

My married life then became a blur of meeting needs: triaging complaints and emergencies, transporting the Lady to appointments with doctors whose medical advice she wouldn't take. Brain MRIs, genetic testing for Alzheimer's, cognitive screenings, back X-rays, nerve burning, pain clinics, hostile opioid tapers, evaluations of unknown skin conditions, spinal fractures, psychiatric drug tapers, knee replacement consultations, cataract surgeries, failed dialectical behavioral therapy groups, failed one-on-one therapy—the list went on and on. If there was a physical, mental, or spiritual problem to be had, the Lady had it.

It's clear to me now that she leveraged her body woes to make up for my moving out of the apartment she and I had shared to start my new life with my husband. The Lady wasn't conscious of that, to be sure. Her mental health prevented her from realizing it. Fred, Lee, and I offered her every resource to be a vibrant elderly person. We tried to calm any inner turmoil she felt by providing external stability—free rent, free car, wellness center memberships, a pool, social encouragement, daily calls, grocery shopping, medication organization, housecleaning, paid bills, weekly visits, church transportation, prepped food, in-home caregiving—but nothing was ever good enough.

"Your mother's never satisfied," King told me when I was four. "It's ah-lah-way-es some-a-thing," he added in his best Gilda Radner impression.

In 2017, seven years after I got married, the Lady died.

The January before her August death, she'd fallen in her condo and broken her arm. Lee's long-term-care insurance provided 24/7 care for her in assisted living, and in February, we moved her in, one mile from our apartment. By August, our mother had perforated diverticulitis and refused surgery. She died two weeks later. The Lady was seventy-seven.

I visited every day she lived there, taking her to the 3:00 P.M. social hour and meals. Eventually she refused to go to either, eating breakfast, lunch, and dinner in her own room and reciting the litany of "undesirables" that ate in the full-service communal dining room. That July, I arranged for her to have daily visits from a physical therapist and occupational therapist, both of whom she fired.

In the parking lot of the nursing home, I got back in my

hot car and banged on the dashboard until I was certain I'd broken my hand.

"Can't you do something about this, God?" I shouted. "How the hell will this ever end? You've got to do something! I can't keep doing this."

Grown children on their way to visit their own parents passed my driver's side window, concerned, but they recognized the frustration. In the steamy car, I saw myself spending the next decade caring for her while she sat in a brand-new blue lift-chair recliner, angry and scratching her scalp off.

And 2017 had been the busiest year of my career. By then, I'd written a few small books for denominational church presses and was traveling to teach at conferences. Much like I had in my sudden and reckless abandonment of my father one month before my wedding, I was just beginning to differentiate from the Lady, and she felt it.

A month after my dashboard screaming match with God, Lee visited. I flew out to Nashville for a book obligation, and he called me a day later to say that Mom was in the intensive care unit for a perforated intestine. Her insides had turned against her, poisoning her body from its center.

She declined surgery, and we all gathered around her to say goodbye. But when she saw the way her family rallied around her in those final days, she told me she was "ready to get back in the saddle."

As it had been the entirety of my life, dealing with the Lady was a constant push-pull, with the swinging highs and lows of "come close and go away," of help-rejecting complaint, of pity party and neediness.

This was the hallmark of both my parents, who were as gifted and capable as they were mentally ill. And I was a midfielder between them, a player whose offensive and defensive duty kept the ball of our lives in play.

My mother's death gave me an opportunity.

With both parents gone, I could decide how I wanted to operate in a world without them. I finally got to call the shots. My autonomy arrived in the form of longing. It tugged at me like a little Indiana girl named Budgie, who pulled on my shirtsleeves and asked me to remember her.

I decided to go home.

The summer after I turned forty, the annual Ernie Pyle festival that Lindah, Doggy, and I had relished as kids returned from a one-year hiatus during the pandemic. Though I'd attended and participated religiously from ages twelve to eighteen, I hadn't been back home to the festival since 2007, three years before King died.

When midwesterners go home after time away, no one makes a fuss. In contrast to over-the-top southern greeters who gush over you like a faulty fire hydrant, Hoosiers are subtle. There is no whooping over family you haven't seen in a week, a year, a decade; Indiana folks who hadn't seen me since King's funeral gave me hugs and said, "Where you been?" like I'd stepped out for a cigarette.

"Alls I know is I haidn't seen yous in a while."

American stereotypes hold in the Midwest. They also hold in the South, Northeast, and West. Even so, Vermillion County isn't full of idiots, people who should be disdained. It's full of people I love. It's full of good corn folks who care about one another. It's full of Hoosiers who have been my angels since the moment King, the Lady, and I returned from Los Angeles to our rightful home.

I remember my first night back at the festival since King died, when we ate homemade noodles served over mashed potatoes with green beans so tender they broke apart on your fork. Men I'd known almost since birth had stirred those beans outside the Dana firehouse since daybreak, toiling over cauldrons to ensure the entire community could eat.

King's good buddies and devotees found me on Main Street, just as they had decades earlier when they cheered me and Lindah and Doggy on as we jitterbugged to Glenn Miller and rode on parade floats that honored veterans like G&GL. Pyro Pete gave me a hug, and I asked him if he remembered his graveside promise to my soon-to-be husband.

"That's a fact," he said. "I'd have killed him if he hurt you. Still would. I don't see nobody," he added with a sigh. With King gone, entourage members had scattered. Some had died off. Others had families and lived decent, straight-edge lives. Viper was long gone, leaving behind only Polaroids of the My Little Pony sleeping bag.

We let our festival bodies with full bellies sag into G&GL's plastic lawn chairs that Uncle Leuge lined up on Main Street in front of the bank where Grandfather had served as president and counted his money with eight fingers. The Regal Grocery Store burned down when my father was still living; G&GL's apartment still stood. Warm light beamed from the living room, where they used to watch TV while they waited for us girls and King to come by and drink brown cows after midnight bike rides. Children of friends we grew up with ran over to our chairs as Uncle Leuge emceed the Friday talent show. Dancing to canned music, the kids glided on the cornstarch spread over spray-painted cakewalk numbers to make rough pavement smooth.

"Where's your shoes?" I heard one of the kids ask another, pointing to their yellow-dusted bare feet.

"Shoes are like coffins for my feet!" the little girl said.

After the talent show, we waited for our names to be called in the merchandise drawing, where Big Ag companies who run the grain elevator soften the nuisance of corn dust by providing prizes for community fundraisers. Our family buys tickets by the hundred dollars' worth to support our town, Ernie's legacy, and the Dana firehouse. Doggy and I won doormats and knives; Uncle Leuge won a rifle and car shampoo. Just before 12:00 A.M., we took Aunt Marietta's golf cart out for a midnight bike ride. Still decorated with Fourth of July shine from the Dollar General, we drove King's old route, past the burning-cop-car alley and Old Man Riley's, up the shit ditch, and back around to Breezo's beating grounds.

The actual town cop, Brewster, passed us at least three times, wondering how we evaded him down alleys. We bumped over potholed asphalt to Steve Dawson's house on the edge of town. When he was sixteen and tan, he wore tank tops and laughed at how we played pool. Now he was alone on his back deck, sipping booze from a silver travel mug.

"Ca-caw, ca-caw," we called out to him, mimicking the gang calls our fathers taught us. Doggy hit the gas and we flew past him.

"Lewman girls!" he shouted, like we were still sixteen.

The next day he stopped us on Main Street, the same cup in his hand, his eyes glassy.

"I knew it was yous. Troublemakers," he said and winked.

Between Uncle Leuge's emceeing responsibilities at the festival, we gathered as a family at the Lewman Museum on Saturday. Lindah and Doggy have kids, and Aunt Marietta now makes them cakes and snack plates. We sat around the kitchen table just like we had decades ago while King and

Leuge taught us the rules of life, starting with the most important: "If you want to murder somebody, you do it in Vermillion County."

"Patch the Pirate still sells out of that good kie-oat pee,"
Uncle Leuge said, unprompted. "It goes for forty-five dollars
a gallon." He said it like it was our loss, then took a bite of
his leftover firehouse chicken-noodle dinner.

"Kie-oats" are coyotes in Vermillion County, mangy canines you sure didn't want to meet in Dog Town.

"Who buys coyote pee?" the girls and I asked in unison,
because that was a more pressing question than why we'd
moved from murder to coyote runoff.

"Hunters," Leuge said. "They love that good kie-oat
piss."

"Do they drink it?" Doggy asked. "I'm cornfused."

Cornfused is our family's term for any perplexing situa-
tion.

Uncle Leuge took a long sip of his Diet Coke. "No," he said.

We waited for clarification.

"Spray themselves," he finally said.

"Oh," we said, as if we knew the ins and outs of shooting
game.

"How does he get their pee?" I asked.

Leuge was silent. His eyes squinted the way they did when
he was studying you.

"There again, this is Vermillion County," Uncle Leuge
said to us, chewing his lunch.

He took another gulp. "Now, girls, I've got exactly one
hour to go to this wedding," he reminded us, changing the
subject again, just like any good Hoosier storyteller. He wiped
his face and left the table, with no further explanation of

Patch's business model of selling coyote pee or how that was tied to the rules of Vermillion County.

It reminded me of how our fathers had always bestowed knowledge on us: bit by bit, spewing scraps alongside rusted trash barrels like racoons. Lindah, Doggy, and I received all our family and life wisdom this way, in this kitchen, on bikes, or in cars, bits and pieces, story shrapnel that refuses tidy narratives because archives are for rich people. But now, only Leuge was here to tell us.

We were ushered to the next festival event, one of Vermillion County's most anticipated weddings. It was being held among the nicest backyards in Dana in the heat of midday, between the pet parade and the cakewalk.

"Bring your own chair," the Nicholses had told everyone.

Doggy and I were late, having changed from our soaked pet parade outfits, or "sweat parade" as Lewmans call it, to midwestern wedding attire, with a coyote pee story in between.

We crossed the alley just as the processional was piped through a Bluetooth speaker.

"Get your asses over there!" A neighbor cupped her hands to her mouth and shouted at us across the crowd. The preacher didn't blink.

The young bride and groom recited their vows as guests shifted in camping chairs and melted in the hot grass. As rows of corn fields framed the scene, we cheered for their love and good fortune in getting married during what Hoosiers in our county considered to be the most auspicious weekend of the year.

The DJ sat under a rented tent. He tested the mic, then silently gazed off toward the crops a hundred feet away. He looked like he relished the moment and had forgotten he was supposed to be doing something else.

A sweet older neighbor who used to sneak us candy cigarettes at the festival greeted me with yellowed eyes. "I'm glad yous's home," he said, squeezing me in a bear hug. I pressed against his poop bag as we embraced. He'd lost weight since the days we took fake drags on the chalky smokes on Main Street.

"UTIs got me," he said, tapping his shit bag.

Another guest sucked on a real cigarette and helped set out more food, swatting the flies that had landed in the fruit. As ash fell into the potato salad, she spoke to the other guests perfectly, as if she'd mastered a side-mouthed Virginia Slim in diapers.

"I told my kids not to eat that," a wedding guest named CJ said, whispering low like her mom, a hilarious grandma who kept the town running and knew all the gossip. CJ was mid-sentence when the melted wedding cake slid off its stand in front of her. She and Doggy dove to catch it with their bare hands. The reception was saved. The lady with the cigarette chuckled, not skipping a beat or a drag.

That night, back at the dusted cakewalk, a band played and we sat with people we'd known our whole lives. Doggy, Lindah, and I told stories about G&GL and recalled King's best midnight bike ride tales. We marveled that hundreds had shown up for this festival when it used to be thousands. We sounded like old people in Vermillion County now, begrudging modernity and reaching for nostalgia. As I looked down Main Street, full of wonder at how there is no place on earth like this town—my namesake—a volunteer fireman held a rifle over his head like it was an Olympic medal. It was being raffled off as a fundraiser for the fire and rescue squad. Another fireman drew the winner.

"Only in Dana," I whispered to Doggy as her kids ran around the cakewalk with townies. But Officer Brewster wasn't even three yards away from the weapon, bulletproof vest on standing watch. *Is it loaded?* I thought. *Surely not.* I'd entered to win it, not because I needed it, but because King taught me "Guns are for idiots," and because I self-righteously imagined that I could keep it out of the hands of someone having a bad day. This was, after all, Vermillion County.

The next morning, I rode the tenth of a mile to Dana Community Bible Church in a late-nineties Mountaineer, Uncle Leuge's favorite vehicle, or "the Death Car" as the girls and I called it. At church, I listened to a guest preacher who posed this question to us: "Why do people believe in evolution?"

"People *actually* believe this all came together like *bang*!" he opened.

I looked around the room.

Belief in evolutionary theory or not, these were my people. These were good folks who cared about this town, this county, and one another. These were folks who were visually impaired but who directed the choir. These were folks who didn't say much outside church but who prayed beautifully aloud in the pews. These were people whom city folks wouldn't trust with their garbage pickup but who faithfully locked up the church every Wednesday and Sunday. These were folks who, year-round, took care of one another through prayer, food, rides, rituals, and a listening ear. These were Vermillion County people who might be outcasts in any other town. These were the people King had taught me to love.

Right there, in the warm sanctuary of Dana Community Bible Church, it dawned on me that the miracle all along was that the Lady had met King in a psychiatric hospital, of all places, where they listened to Dr. Schuller and were convinced to pack up everything to move to L.A. and sit at his feet, eager for their own miracle.

The miracle was that they'd gotten their baby girl and that we'd all survived the Ninth Street trailer, Carnival Captivations, knives and guns, hot-box torture, car wrecks, mental illness, and psychotic breaks. We'd survived homelessness and bankruptcy and loss and addiction. King had survived a Vermillion County upbringing. I had too.

I thought of King and the Lady and the finitude of an hour—and a life. "There's only so much sugar in the sack, Budge," King had always said.

He was right.

The wonder of it all was that we'd had time enough. I'd reached adulthood, thanks to my parents and every other person from Indiana to North Carolina who'd made sure I was safe and cared for.

I'd emerged from this battlefield—its dirt and people and weapons and stories and wounds and rage—not unscathed but stronger. Courageous. Tenacious. Unbroken. Amid the casings of these blown-up lives, mine included, I uncovered healing and home in the very place where "you can get away with murder." It turns out that this place—Vermillion County, western Indiana—was my home all along.

"A person never really misses a little town such as Dana until he's actually away for a while," King had said.

I'd been missing it for far too long.

Just as it's true that a preschooler's hands are the perfect size for razor blades, it's also true that helping my schizophrenic drug-lord father chop, drop, and traffic kilos in kiddie-ride carcasses across flyover country was the best thing that ever happened to me.

I realize now that the real danger of my drug-trafficking childhood wasn't the weapons or the fight training or the drug business. It wasn't King's schizophrenic psychosis or the Lady's personality disorders.

The real danger was denying what happened between two trailers. The real danger was in not accepting my parents for who they were, mental illness and addiction and poverty and all. The real danger was in not realizing that they were doing the very best they could with what they had.

The real danger was in hiding it all.

Maybe King was right: You can't fix crazy. Or better yet, maybe you don't need to. Because trying to means that you spend your entire life thinking you are adrift, which leaves you secretive, ashamed, isolated, confused, wandering, and lonely, as Budgie or Revy, depending on the day. When, in fact, you are really *both*.

Home, it turns out, was there all along in my two very loving *and* very unconventional yet faithful parents, who believed in miracles.

I am their miracle.

I am their legacy.

They are my home.

Home, it turns out, is where the war is. It's also where the healing begins.

| ACKNOWLEDGMENTS |

BETWEEN TWO TRAILERS HAS HAD MANY EARLY CHEERLEAD-ers who deserve much gratitude. Of them, Evan Derkacz and Lisa Webster were the first. Donna Freitas and Lauren Winner too.

The Collegeville Institute and Louisville Institute supported this book project and its podcast version, *Breaking Good*. Bridget Sidi's editorial precision and curiosity helped focus and form the book proposal and early chapters.

Thanks to Mark Bennett and Yonat Shimron, who were the first to write about this story publicly, with a particular focus on how the town of Dana, Indiana, and small corn towns like it face issues of food insecurity, housing insecurity, poverty, addiction, and mental illness. Their articles helped shed light on neglected issues in Big Agriculture's Middle America. Much gratitude goes to Mike Mather, DeAmon Harges, and Brian Williams—whose spiritual care of Indiana communities inspired my work. Special thanks to the town of Dana and Sara Benskin for sharing the vision of how small towns can leverage their already-present resources to improve their residents' quality of life. Countless others provided key details and corroborated events that gave the story its credibility and vividness. You know who you are; I am more grateful than I can convey here.

Early endorsers of this project—Barbara Brown Taylor, Sarah Edmondson, Jonathan Merritt, Carine McCandless, and Philip Gulley—were gracious in lending their time and kind words.

And it was Mark Tauber, agent extraordinaire, who believed in this book so wholeheartedly from the start. His enthusiasm and wisdom found it the perfect home at Convergent with Keren Baltzer at the helm. Keren understood the book's voice—and its purpose—from paragraph one. Special thanks to Jocelyn Kiker and Kayla Fenstermaker, who shepherded the text and fine-tuned clumsy words with sharp edits. And, finally, thank you to Leita Williams and the entire Convergent team at Penguin Random House for their care and keen vision for how to share this story with readers wrestling with the meaning of home.

In addition to family, a tight circle of friends kept me grounded while proposing, drafting, and revising: Erin Lane, Rush Beam, Kate Harris, Stephanie Austria, Joanna Kennedy, Barbara Jessie-Black, Heather Sanderson, Kyle Hager, Priya Gopal, Mahamantra Das, Gopalnandini Lipscomb, Diane Faires, Michael Beadle, Sharon Cummings, Sally Bates, Mary June Jones, Laurie Holden, Citta Hari Brown, Jennifer Hege, Kristin Krupp, Madeline Day, Sharon Seyfarth Garner, Whitney Simpson, and Kristen Vincent.

Achilles, Uncle Leuge, Aunt Marietta, Lindah, and Doggy: Thank you for your support as I swam my way through. When I was drowning, you saved me. You are my solid shore.

And Fred, husband of the century, love across lifetimes: It's always been you.

Finally, thanks to all those readers who long for home and took the time to explore it here with me. May you have found a morsel of it among these pages—and within yourself.

ABOUT THE AUTHOR

AUTHOR + TEACHER + GOOD BUDDY

J. DANA TRENT is an unlikely Hoosier and professor of religion and critical thinking in Raleigh,
North Carolina. She is a graduate of Duke Divinity School and an ordained minister in the Baptist
tradition. She's made her father proud by being a
good buddy and pleased her mother by being a
helpful reverend. Dana copes with life by moving
and making lists, two skills she learned from King
and the Lady, respectively. She and her vegetarian
husband, Fred, have two cats.

Between Two Trailers is J. Dana Trent's debut
trade memoir.